£8

The First Three Y

Karl König

The First Three Years of the Child

Floris Books

First published in German under the title
Die ersten drei Jahre des Kindes
by Verlag Freies Geistesleben, Stuttgart, 1957

© Verlag Freies Geistesleben, Stuttgart, 1957
Second English edition published in 2004 by Floris Books

British Library CIP Data available

ISBN 0-86315-452-2

Printed in Great Britain
by The Bath Press, Bath

Contents

Introduction

During the first three years of his earthly existence man acquires those faculties that enable him to become a human being. In the course of the first year he learns to walk, during the second he acquires speech, and during the third, he experiences the awakening of thought. He is born as a helpless infant and only by acquiring these three faculties of walking, speaking and thinking does he grow into a being who can name himself, gain free mobility and, with the help of speech, come into conscious communication with his fellow men in the surrounding world. A kind of threefold miracle happens because here is revealed more than instinct, more than adaptation, more than the unfolding of inherited faculties.

The acquisition of the three fundamental human faculties is an act of grace that is bestowed on every human being. It is also a process of extraordinary complexity. Only a closer study of these phenomena reveals how manifold and varied are the ways in which the whole human being is woven into this developmental process.

The following deliberations try to follow the traces on the path that leads to learning to walk, speak and think. A concluding chapter is concerned with how the interaction of these three fundamental soul faculties work into one another and are connected with the three highest senses: the senses of speech, thought and self or ego.

Chapter 1

Acquisition of the Ability to Walk Upright

The processes of movement

The faculty of walking upright is part of the phenomenon of the whole human organization's faculty of movement, and it is quite one-sided to assume that we use mainly our legs and feet for walking. The entire bodily apparatus of movement is used for walking and the arms are engaged as much as the legs. The muscles of the back and chest are as intimately involved as are those that move the eyeballs.

It is necessary to recognize that the whole human being is engaged in every movement he makes because the movement of one part of his body presupposes the state of rest of the other parts that are not actively engaged in this movement. During waking hours from morning until night, the resting condition of some parts of the body is never a passive but always an active function. This points to an archetypal phenomenon of all movement. If one part of the bodily apparatus of movement is in motion, then the remaining part is engaged in such a way that through an active state of rest the mobility of the other part is made possible.

When I bend my arm, then I must, in order to make this flexion possible, not only actively relax the extensors of the arm in question, but all other muscles must form an active abutment to counter-balance this flexion. Thus, it is always the whole motor apparatus that takes part in every movement and helps in its performance.

The involvement of the whole bodily apparatus of movement

can be experienced directly when, for example, a toe is hindered in its ability to move freely through an injury. Immediately the function of the whole foot is arrested and the movement of the leg is changed, all of which leads indirectly to a different use of the remaining motor system. How often do pains gradually occur in the muscles of the neck and spine when a foot cannot be used properly for walking, and how often can a change in the rhythm of breathing be observed when a leg must be kept quiet for a long time. These are simple examples, but they clearly show what appears as a first and fundamental phenomenon in the realm of movement. It can be formulated as follows:

1. The entire bodily apparatus of movement is a functional unity. Its elements never move as independent members but each movement occurs in the realm of the bodily motor system.
2. Therefore, the parts in motion show merely an apparent independence in contrast to those at rest. The resting parts, however, participate as actively in the process of movement as the parts in motion, even if this is not immediately evident.

Recognition of the bodily motor organization as a functional unity has been prevented by the dominance of the concept of localization of the control of movement in the central nervous system. This is the result of the analytical method of scientific thinking of the nineteenth century and in our time would best be overcome. As little as single letters alone give meaning to the word, or single words the sentence, just as little does a series of single muscles move a limb of the body. The pattern of a movement uses muscles singly and in groups and so the movement is made apparent. Just as, when an opinion is stated, use is made of the sentence, which in turn takes its form from spoken words, so does gesture fall into single patterns of movement that call on groups of muscles to execute what the gesture demands.

When I feel repulsion, various patterns of movement are at the disposal of this feeling. These patterns select specific groups of muscles from the whole motor apparatus and execute a movement with them in which the whole apparatus participates. Desire and repulsion, sympathy and antipathy, anger and anxiety, fear and courage, all have their corresponding forms of movement. More refined feelings and sensations such as listening and devotion, joy and pain, weeping and laughing also have gesture patterns at their disposal and service. When man learns to write or weave, to carve, paint, hammer or forge, he has himself acquired movement patterns that are thus his own creation. These are not given to him as part of his heritage as a created being.

The most fundamental of these acquired forms of movement, a gesture permeating the whole of human life, is the ability to walk upright. In standing erect man raises himself to a position that continually demands that he come to terms with the earth's gravity. The four-legged animal is in a greater state of equilibrium with gravity, but man must learn to stay uninterruptedly erect. He must not only rest freely in his uprightness, but also be able to move unburdened.

How does he acquire this faculty that demands his constant personal involvement?

The development of human walking

The child's ability to move does not begin after birth but already exists during fetal development. From the end of the second month of pregnancy onward, movements of the fetus can be detected, and in the course of the fifth month they become so strong that the mother can perceive them.

After birth, the child possesses a general mobility from which certain specific forms of movement stand out. Soon after birth, for example, he can perform perfect sucking movements when the breast is offered. He can also, from the time of his birth, control his breathing. Repulsion brought about by fear causes movement, and completely aimless and uncoordinated kicking movements as expressions of well-being are distributed over the whole body. Stern describes these movements as spontaneous and points out that they occur in a dissociated fashion. 'Many newborn infants,' he writes, 'can move each eye independently of the other. One may turn up, the other out, or one may remain stationary while the other looks down.'[1]

Stern calls attention in particular to eye movements because their coordination takes place remarkably quickly. 'It is true,' he continues, 'that this period [of dissociated eye movements] passes quickly, sometimes even at the moment of birth, so that such children appear to have been born with coordinated eye movements.'

Controlled eye movements thus stand out from the general chaos of kicking movements even during the first days of life. This is the beginning, however, of the process of movement that will be completed at the end of the first year when the child has learned to walk. In learning to walk he acquires his first mastery over space. But the acquisition of this faculty proceeds according to a definitely ordered sequence that starts at the head and neck and gradually extends downward to the chest, arms, back, and finally to the legs and feet. Generally speaking, the child learns to master movements of the head and neck during the first three months after birth. During the second quarter, he controls lifting his arms and hands. These movements can be distinguished from the general kicking, so he can now be called, a little grasper. In this way, by the end of this period he has learned to sit freely. In the third quarter the child discovers his legs and begins to practice standing. During the last quarter he carries his ability to stand over into his first free steps and experiences his feet as organs touching the ground. The first conquest of space has thus been completed.

The developmental process of movement, therefore, is shifted from the head down over the chest and legs into the feet, following a course through the body from above downwards. It becomes evident when we ask the meaning of this that it directly conditions the erect body posture. The head is the first member to withdraw from chaotic movement. Chest and arms are pulled along after it, and finally the legs and feet extricate themselves. This process seems to be patterned after that of actual birth. Just as in birth the head is the first part of the body to emerge and is gradually followed by the rest of the body, so here, out of the womb of dissociated movements, coordinated movement is born and oriented step by step toward standing and walking. At the end of the first year the process of the birth of movement is completed.

With this achievement the head is directed upward and the

feet touch the earth. The head acquires a position of rest, a fact to which Rudolf Steiner has drawn attention time and again, and is suspended lightly upon the shoulders, becoming the resting point around which the movement of the limbs can take place.

The fundamental investigations of Magnus and de Kleijn[2] on the attitudinal and positional reflexes have shown the central position taken by the neck and head muscles in early development. The head takes an independent position of rest in order to make possible a free and harmonious mobility of the limbs. This applies especially to the ability to walk. When a human being can keep his head upright and still, he has also learned to walk. As long as an individual's head is restless and wobbly in the totality of movement, normal walking cannot be attained.

After the first year the child also learns to free his arms from the action of walking and to use them independently. This happens because the head gradually becomes fixed and consolidated in its position of rest and is able to confront the free play of the limbs independently. The head, therefore, is a centre resting within the movements of the body.

What has been said here can be summed up as follows. A child learns to walk in stages and gives birth to his motility from the head downwards out of the chaos of early movement. As a result, the head attains a position of rest as opposed to the free mobility of the limbs. Once an upright position has been achieved, the limbs must constantly come to terms with the gravitational forces of space because man, as an upright being, must be able to assume a freely mobile position of equilibrium rather than one that is fixed.

Separation of self and world

It has been pointed out that coordination of eye movements is achieved immediately after birth when the child acquires the first rudiments of what later becomes his ability to look and the actions connected with it. The eyes learn to turn to definite points in the outside world.

When we consider that in coordinating eye movements the first fixed point in the relationship between the soul and its surroundings is established, the fundamental importance of seeing as a human act becomes still more evident. It is by means of our eyes that we try to establish a conscious relationship with our surroundings even during the first days of our earthly life. This is not to say that the child can already perceive, but he begins to explore the surrounding world as it is gradually revealed by the 'touch' of his gaze. In this way a first dull sensation of the 'there' in contrast to the 'self' comes about. In the course of the first year the dull feeling will slowly brighten and gradually lead to the contrast between the sensation of his own body and that of the surrounding world, but the outside and inside, the there and the here, will still be completely interwoven. Adalbert Stifter has expressed this period of development in his autobiographical fragment as follows.

> Far back in the empty void, something like rapture and delight entered my being, mightily grasping it as if to destroy. I can compare it to nothing else in my later life. What I remember was glory, turmoil; it was below. This must have occurred very early in my childhood because it seems to me as if a dark nothingness, high and broad, lay around about it. Then there was something else that passed gently and soothingly through my inner being, which I can now characterize as sound. I swam in something that fanned me. I swam to and fro and it became softer and softer within me until I became as if drunk. Then there was nothing more. These demi-islands of remembrance lie in the veiled ocean of the past, fairylike and legendary, like the primeval memories of a people.[3]

Gradually the child's dull consciousness, which consists of merging sense perceptions and feelings, is lit up as the world becomes differentiated from his body. The process of differentiation, however, starts with the child's looking about. As his gaze gradually becomes fixed, the individual forms of the environment can be gropingly touched and grasped. Around the focus of looking, the head emerges as a structure belonging to the self. The baby learns to lift his head and to use it as an organ of orientation, turning it to where light, colour, sound or smell come to meet him.

As time goes on, the child's eyes catch sight more often of his little hands and fingers playing and moving in front of them. When not only his eyes, but also his hands begin to grasp objects, holding and dropping them again, then the trunk, including arms and hands, stands out as a whole against the world. At this time the child has acquired the faculty of sitting freely and in doing so, he has already achieved a good deal. His head is suspended above his body and can be freely turned. His eyes begin to extend their gaze further into space while his hands grasp closer things and bring them to his mouth, etc. His hands now can also grasp the edge of the cradle. They can hold on to it, and he can pull his body up.

Then the great moment occurs when, at about the end of the ninth month, the child pulls himself up by himself into an upright position for the first time. A decisive step has been taken in the separation of world and body. The surrounding world has separated itself from the child and it confronts the selfhood, which now comprehends the world as something alien. The new self, however, begins to move within this separated world by crawling, sliding and pushing. Every day and every hour new impressions appear, always quickly forgotten and always freshly conquered. The many new experiences demand to be seized, grasped, beheld and touched. Thus, the circle of forms coming into shape enters into action for the first time. The senses ask for mobility, and movement in turn conquers new sense experiences. At this time, this process is quite obvious.

At last the child, now in an upright position, can take his first uncertain steps. The pride of the parents often cannot be compared with the child's joy in what he has achieved. The world, no longer strange and uncanny, turns into something that can be conquered by a freely moving being. By achieving his first step as an upright being the child has also taken his first step away from being a creature to becoming a creator. Stern expresses it as follows:

So, towards the end of the first year, the spadework in the mastery of actual space is mainly accomplished. The child can grasp the spatial features of things — their position,

distance, shape and size — and he accommodates himself
to them. He distinguishes far and near, great and small,
round and angular, above and below, before and behind
— in short, he has roughly a perception of space, which
certainly is still capable of many misconceptions and will
need in years to come to be refined, made clearer and
developed, but not enriched with any intrinsically new
features.[4]

Space perception comes about at the end of the first year only
because the child can experience the above and below by the
development of his ability to stand erect. He has experienced
what is near and far by his movements, the round and angular
by his touch, and various positions in space by his gaze. But all
this happens only because the process of separation between self
and world had been completed. The child does not learn to walk
by learning to bring certain muscular movements under control. He begins to control movements through a waking of consciousness that gradually brings the body to stand out from its
environment as a separate self. The delivery of the body from
the intimate embrace of its mothering environment leads to the
ability to walk erect. Walking erect is not a simple process of
movement that makes locomotion possible. Learning to walk
reveals a process of developing consciousness that leads to the
perception of the environment as something 'outside.' The
process begins with 'looking,' continues in grasping and culmi-
nates in walking. The awakening consciousness that enables the
child to comprehend his own self at the end of the first year
moves from the *gaze* of the eye over the *grasp* of the hands to the
step of the feet.

    The inner meaning of walking can only be understood when
we see it in its entirety. We can walk upright because it is possible for us to develop from creatures woven into the world fabric
to individual beings confronting the world.

Inherited and acquired movements

As a result of important investigations, Portmann has pointed
out that the first year of human life is of special significance in

that the development that takes place in humans during this period occurs in other mammals within the uterus. Setting this first year apart from the later periods of the child's development, he calls it the 'extra-uterine spring season.' He says, 'The newborn child can be called a "secondary" nestling because, considering the extent of his development, he is really a fledgling without, however, having acquired a fledgling's free mobility.'[5] The extent of man's development at birth indicates his special position in the realm of the living. Portmann somehow divines these inherent evolutionary problems.

Portmann also quotes Stirnimann's investigations, which must be considered in relation to the findings mentioned earlier concerning the positional and attitudinal reflexes of the child. These are known to be spontaneous activities of the newborn child that occur in response to certain circumstances of stress. Thus, the child shows that it is possible for him to stand, crawl and walk during the first months. These incipient faculties, however, are lost by the fifth month, thereby making it possible for him to achieve proper crawling, standing and walking from the ninth month on.

> To be prepared to stand, one must possess the ability to place his limbs in the standing position. To demonstrate this in the newborn child different parts of the body surface or the eyes must be stimulated. Held upright, for example, even the newborn child tends to stretch his legs when the soles of his feet come in contact with a firm surface. He does not yet show any clear readiness to stand, however, but is only capable of performing the action when his legs have been brought into the proper position. During the second quarter of the year, a readiness to stand occurs when the *upper* part of the child's foot is touched. When, for example, he is held upright so that the upper part of his foot touches the lower edge of a table-top, he will bend first one leg and then the other. Then, putting the sole of his foot on the table, he will straighten his leg out and will finally stand with both feet on the table.

... It is possible to induce reflex walking movements in all normal, healthy newborn babies. To demonstrate this, the child is held around the waist with both hands, and is stood upright on a firm base. Certain supporting reactions in the legs result. If his body is now tilted slightly forward, he will make proper walking movements and take steps if he is moved in keeping with them. He will have a tendency to cross his legs, but nevertheless steps of about four inches each will be taken. In the course of further development, around the end of the first six months, these walking movements recede into the background and so cannot be said to represent an immediate preparatory step to true walking.

... J. Bauer has described something similar as a crawling phenomenon. If one puts a small baby belly-down on a table and supports the soles of his feet with his hands, the baby begins to crawl by pushing himself away from the supporting hands. The arms are lifted and placed forward one after the other, and in this way the child can be made to crawl across the table. According to Bauer, the crawling phenomenon occurs only in the first four months and then only when the child lies on its belly.

In these quotations is characterized the three most important achievements of spontaneous movement in the child that occur before he acquires the ability to stand and walk upright. It is of the utmost significance to the proper course of later develop-ment that these movements appear during the first months after birth and then disappear, thus making possible their reappear-ance later in a completely new metamorphosis as crawling, standing and walking.

Without referring to the particular investigations mentioned above, O. Storch has reported two forms of movement that he calls 'inherited and acquired motor movements' (*Erbmotorik und Erwerbsmotorik*).[6] Although in the case of the child one can hardly speak of inherited motor actions being manifested during the first months, congenital movements must nonetheless be differentiated from those acquired by learning, of which walking is the most important.

The findings of Förster and C. and O. Vogt are also relevant. They state that premature and occasionally also fully mature babies show movements that may be described as typically athetotic. 'The movements can be described as follows. The arms are bent at the elbows at right angles, the lower arms turned strongly out so that the palms face outward, while the wrists are stretched or even over-stretched against the lower arms. Simultaneously, these babies play a strange game of stretching, bending and spreading their fingers and toes out by stretching or overstretching them all at once or one after the other.'

In the course of the first months these choreatic-athetotic movements pass over into general kicking, which in turn is gradually overcome so that by the end of the first year walking has been learned.

Athetotic children, however, who because of certain brain injuries do not learn to walk or do so only with difficulty, show symptoms that clearly and unequivocally point to the forms of movement just described. A child with the characteristic symptoms of Little's disease shows the same *pes equinus* position and the tendency to cross his legs when trying to walk. Thus, in these children, the movements of early childhood described above continue into later life and present the symptomatology of grave motor disturbances. Such abnormalities cannot be overcome because walking as an acquired motor activity cannot redeem the persisting inherited movements.

Children who cannot develop the reflexes of position and attitude show the crawling phenomena described above. This group, whose disturbances belong to the forms of cerebellar ataxis, remain crawlers throughout life because they cannot acquire the ability to walk upright owing to the failure of their sense of equilibrium.

The so-called athetotics retain the forms of movement associated with premature birth and these then lead to serious disturbances of posture and movement. Here, above all, the directed and ordered movements are disturbed, but the ability to walk upright can be acquired gradually by quite a few children in this group.

In athetotic children the range of motor disturbances is not a pathological condition that arises anew. These disturbances are rather the physiological remnants of the behaviour patterns of early childhood. The inability to learn to walk upright is common to all of these children because of the retention of early movement patterns that later assume disproportionate dimensions. What has been described earlier in this chapter as the birth of walking out of the chaos of general movement cannot be accomplished by them.

A retardation is also shown in the general attitude of these child patients. The lighting up of consciousness that follows the differentiation between self and world, or between body and environment, while walking is being learned, does not take place. The athetotic child can hardly master his feelings and suffers from an erratic, unruly occurrence of laughing and weeping that is beyond his control.

The spastic child suffering from Little's disease is so completely given over to his sense impressions that he cannot control them, or at best does so only with difficulty. A slight noise makes him wince and a strong light intensifies his muscle spasms. This makes any development in space almost impossible for these children, based as it must be on the experience of 'there' and 'here.'

The behaviour of those children who cannot attain positional and attitudinal reflexes also shows that they cannot retain sense impressions. The development of memory occurs only involuntarily, and they are hardly able consciously to call up memories at the right occasion.

From these brief indications it can be seen how fundamentally important walking is for the soul-development of man. If walking fails to develop, then the control of feelings and moods is missing, the conscious use of the faculty of memory is lacking, and separation of self and world is not achieved.

If we did not learn to walk, further development of the conscious unfolding of the specific human faculties in the course of childhood would not be possible. The way leading to school is in reality open only to those children who can go walking upright. For the others, measures of curative education can compensate for what they have had to forego in the development of the first year even though learning to walk, as an act of grace, could not become manifest in them.

If, in an understanding of the uprightness of man, one does not include the observations touched upon here, then the following remark of Portmann can be readily understood. 'The true meaning of the slow development of the completely upright position of the body, and the bodily structure basic to this position, can still hardly be grasped.'[7] Only he, however, cannot grasp it who looks at man's ability to walk upright as simple locomotion and lacks the courage to admit the fundamental difference that exists between the upright position of man and that of the higher animals. Endowed as they are with a horizontally oriented spine, the animals remain part of the world. They are overwhelmed by sense impressions and the abyss between self and world does not open. In them the head is not carried above the spine as if floating, but remains incompletely differentiated as a continuation, not yet a separate creation, at the anterior end of the body. Memory pictures, therefore, can only be retained, but not recalled. Pleasure and displeasure, greed and disgust, constantly changing, flood the inner experiences. The upright posture alone causes the abyss to open between self and world, and this leads to the further acquisition of speech and thought.

The ability to stand, the reflex walking movements, crawling and the athetotic movements of premature births differ fundamentally from the new phenomenon of walking. They must disappear in the course of the first year to make walking possible. Whether these archetypal movements are called inherited or congenital or whether they are attributed to activities of certain nerve centres of the cerebrum or cerebellum, is not as important as to recognize the entirely new impulse brought forth in the acquisition of walking.

From the development of looking and grasping on to the acquisition of walking, a new power unfolds, opposing all biological processes. This force first takes hold of the eyes, bring the axes of sight into line, and thus makes possible the fixation of the gaze. It directs the arms and hands of the body toward purposeful movements, and the hands learn to grasp, to fold and to hold each other. Finally, the soles of the feet touch the ground. From the heels to the toes they enter the field of gravity — something that does not happen with any animal — and the head is lifted, reaching into the light. In this picture of the upright position is presented the polarity of light and gravity.

Thus a new element enters that must be realized as the member of the human being that can be attributed only to man and to no other creature on earth. Rudolf Steiner calls this entity, 'I.' Through his 'I' every human being can receive the gift of grace of walking. When it appears in the form of uprightness, all other forms of movement recede and disappear. It is as if the shepherd enters among the herd, and the herd then grows quiet and restful, gathering around him.

In this way, all other forms of movement arrange themselves around the power of uprightness, which, in the moment it appears, brings order and guidance with it.

The year and the stages of learning to walk upright

Now that we have attempted to approach those phenomena connected with the acquisition of the upright walk in a special way, a strange conformity to law is revealed during this period that should be mentioned. It can hardly be mere chance that it takes approximately a year to learn to walk and that development that is premature or retarded is expressed symptomatically as a disturbance in the unfolding of the child's being. To learn to walk takes the same amount of time as that required by the earth to circle the sun, which suggests that this sun-earth rhythm is inscribed in this human faculty.

Rudolf Steiner has pointed out that man acquires his uprightness here on earth as something entirely new. 'It is significant,' he says, 'that man should have to work upon himself in order to make a being that can walk erect out of one that cannot walk at all. It is man who gives himself his vertical stance and his equilibrium in space.'[8] This earthly acquisition of the ability to walk is placed in the cosmic time relationship between sun and earth.

A study of the gradual progress of this year of learning to walk can be expressed as a calendar that has been worked out by a number of observers and shows approximately the following stages:

1st month: The child's eyes begin to fix their gaze.

2nd month: Even when lying belly-down, the child begins to hold his head upright.

3rd month: When placed belly-down, the child can lift his shoulders together with his head, and keep them elevated for a time.

4th month: When placed belly-down, he can support himself on the palms of his hands. He grasps a new situation with active gaze. He begins to reach for objects that he has found by touch. In the act of grasping he can bring both hands together without using his fingers.

5th month: While lying on his back, he can lift his head and shoulders. He has learned to turn from his back onto his side, and he is also able to grasp with his hands objects he has seen.

6th month: The child is able to sit up with support. He can bring a movable object into contact with a resting one. He can, for example, beat rhythmically with a spoon upon a table.

7th month: The child begins to move away from a position of rest. He tries to get desired objects and to reach them by changing his position.

8th month: He now sits independently and begins to crawl.

9th month: The child learns to raise himself to a sitting position without support. He learns to kneel and begins to stand with support.

10th month: He is able to throw things.

11th month: The child can raise himself and stand by holding on to something.

12th month: He can stand freely and with a little help and support take his first steps.

If one reads this calendar of the first year not only as a schema showing the 'intelligence' of the growing baby, but also tries to live through what happens, then these twelve months become the true course of a year in which the acquired faculties stand out individually like festivals.

Rudolf Steiner has said that in earlier epochs of human evolution birth always took place during Christmas time.[9] This
remained so up to the third millennium BC, especially among
the North Germanic tribes. Births only gradually began to
spread out over the whole year. Thus it was formerly true that
children first saw the light of the world at a definite time of the
year. Gradually, in the course of the further development of
mankind, this link with nature was abolished.

Accordingly, learning to walk in former times was accomplished in the year between one Christmas and the next and, as
if into the milestones of incarnations that remained from this,
the various festivals were inscribed. These were celebrated first
as pre-Christian and later as Christian festivals. While the following correspondences cannot be 'explained' in the ordinary
sense, it is left to the individual to try to experience the connections resulting from them.

It may be significant that the baby smiles for the first time
and can lift his head from the horizontal just at the time when
the festival of the presentation in the Temple, Candlemas, is
celebrated.

At Easter, the baby learns to hold up his head and shoulders
while on his belly; he raises himself so to speak above the water.
He reaches for objects, answers a look with a smile and touches
things. His arms are freed.

Around Whitsun, he can grasp an object he sees and thus
coordinates his hands and eyes. He can turn from a back to a
side position, freeing himself from the base on which he lies.

At St John's tide the child sits up. Now the sun stands at
the highest point of the heavens, and as a human being, the
child holds his head freely above his horizontal shoulders.

At Michaelmas he sits up by himself and learns to kneel and
to stand by supporting himself.

At the beginning of Advent, the child puts himself freely into
space, and by Christmas he can take his first, hesitant steps.
Now a creature is on his way to becoming a creator.

★ ★ ★

These hints have been given to help those who seek a new understanding of man, not to open the gates to mystic speculation. We should practice such thoughts and cultivate the feelings arising from them especially when watching children to whom the ability to walk has been denied. Then a new power to help will call forth the will and bring help where help is otherwise denied. In every child who learns to walk today these words are at work: 'Arise! Take up thy bed and walk!' It is the sun power that raises the earthly body of man so he can walk erect over the earth.

Chapter 2

Learning One's Native Language

Speech as expression, naming and speaking

After the child has become able to raise himself to an erect position and acquires free mobility in space, the second step in becoming man follows. He learns to speak and use his native language. This is an especially impressive acquisition and only in recent decades have child psychologists paid deserving attention to its importance. By the time the child learns to speak his native language by conquering words and word connections, he has taken a most important step on the path toward becoming man. The tremendous gulf separating man and animal is also indicated here. Portmann is fully justified in saying, 'Therefore, we must point emphatically to the fact that human speech in word as well as gesture, both of which rest on the principle of communication through signs, is something totally different from all animal sounds.'[1]

Those animal sounds when made by man are also only sound. Cries, screams, moans or other sounds expressing the woes and joys of existence are not speech. Speech is not merely expression, but naming. One of the roots of speech is to be found in the fact that through it *names* are given to the world and its manifestations.

In the First Book of Moses you can read,

> So out of the ground the Lord God formed every beast of
> the field, and every bird of the air, and brought them to
> the man to see what he would call them; and whatever
> the man called every living creature, that was its name.
> And the man gave names to all cattle, and to the birds of

the air, and to every beast of the field; but for the man
there was not found an helper fit for him. (Gen. 2:19f).

The giving of names is directly connected with the creation of
Eve. With whom, after all, should man speak if not with his own
kind? He can give names to the animals. He can name things
and beings, but who is to answer when he begins to ask? The
word spoken into space remains without an answer, is shattered
and blown away. It dies, and dumbness follows.

These brief remarks hint at the soul qualities that form
speech and speaking. Only a small part of speech is an expression of human existence and feeling, and as such it is still intimately connected with man's animal nature. When, however,
through speech, sounds are raised out of this sphere and the
tones humanized, speech then becomes the servant of the word.
The sounding tone unites with the power of speech and thus
the names of things can be pronounced. It is speech itself working through man that calls things by name.

This, however, is not all. Naming is only the statement of
fact. Speech strives for something more; it aims at finding a connection with itself. Speech wants to come to terms with the
word that is heard in order to understand what it has heard, to
answer the question received, to demand answers from out of
its own questioning. Therefore, God gives Adam his Eve
because only when man experiences himself through speech in
another human being does he become aware of himself.

Speech can now be said to unfold in the human being in a
threefold manner:

1. As an expression of what lives in the soul as animality.
2. As an expression of the ability to name all things of this
    world. Thus, the names of things and beings sound forth.
3. As an expression of the power that tries to meet itself in
    speaking. Speech thereby gradually comes to terms with
    itself.

Man is connected with this threefold expression of speech
through his whole being. At first, however, he is not the one

who speaks, but the one through whom speech sounds and expresses itself. For this it needs its own tools and these are created in man by speech itself. The immature man represents an undeveloped natural condition in which speech becomes active in such a way that it is able to become manifest. Even as the artist creates tools from the substances of nature by means of which he fashions his work, so speech takes man as the natural substance and creates out of him its own work of art. Thus, man ultimately appears as image because through the speech with which he has been endowed, he can become manifest as self. He can sound through it (*personare*) as personality and communicate with, or impart himself to other human beings.

It was a rather childish agnosticism that imagined and also tried to prove that the organs of speech were no more than the larynx with which, when speaking, some small parts of the cerebral cortex are connected, and that these are the essential elements through which man begins to prattle. Today we know that it is the whole of man who speaks. As physical, soul and spirit being he takes part in the formation of speech and in speaking expresses himself as personality. Rudolf Steiner has described it in the following way:

> It is in the form of the larynx and all that is connected with it that makes us man ... All the rest of the human form, down to the smallest details, has been so formed and plastically moulded that at the present stage man is, so to speak, a further elaboration of his organs of speech. The organs of speech are fundamental to the human form.[2]

What are these instruments of human speech, whose further formation and metamorphosis man himself seems to be?

The anatomy of the organs of speech

The larynx, the centre of the organs of speech, is the intricately formed, central part of a pipe through which the breath streams in and out. This pipe, which widens and branches out downward as well as upward, is called the trachea or windpipe. Air passes down through the windpipe, then through the two large bronchi that enter the right and left lobes of the lungs. As these tubes penetrate the lungs further, they continue to divide dichoto-mously, growing smaller and smaller, multiplying over and over again. The final configuration, rightly called 'bronchial tree,' is formed like the trunk of a tree that divides into two main branches. These divide further into smaller ones, finally forming twigs and ever smaller twigs. The only difference between the trunk of this tree and that of an ordinary one is that its roots are in the larynx and its branches grow downward. Thus, this bronchial tree is upside-down compared to natural trees.

Just as each twig of a tree terminates in a leaf, so each of the innumerable bronchioli terminates in an alveolus, a small cell into which the inhaled air streams. There the air meets indi-rectly the blood that flows around the walls of the alveolus. The inhaled air, changed through this meeting, streams back in exha-lation and passes once more through the larynx on its way out. While being breathed out the air gives service to speech. The laryngeal muscles rhythmically move the parts of the larynx, creating a thickening and thinning of the outstreaming air, which forms the pliable basic substance needed for the forma-tion of tone and sound.

The pipe around which the larynx is formed also continues upward as the pharynx, or throat, that opens into the oral and nasal cavities. From the throat, two small Eustachian tubes lead backward to the middle ear to connect indirectly with the air vesicles of the temporal bone lying behind.

The mouth, including teeth, lips, tongue, cheeks and palate, is the sculptor of the sounds of speech. It moulds the air pre-pared by the larynx to form labial, palatal, dental and lingual sounds, and can cause the prepared air to be aspirated or forced, vibrated or nasalized. From these various combinations the con-sonants are formed.

The nasal cavity acts as a resonator. It also regulates the amount of air needed.

The Eustachian tubes leading to the middle ear create an intimate connection between speaking and hearing that should not be over looked.

To arrive at a real and concrete picture of this structure, we would have to say: Proceeding downward, the trunk of the windpipe opens into the two large bronchi. These then continually divide and finally become the innumerable air cells, or alveoli, of the lungs. The alveoli, like tender organs of touch, meet the expanding plane of the surrounding blood. So it is that in the lungs the air of the speech organs experiences the touch of the flowing blood. Like so many thousands of little feet, the alveoli touch the surface of the blood, feel its strength or weakness, its speed or hesitancy. They are thus a vastly extended organ of touch that experiences the nature of the blood and reacts accordingly. It is for this reason that we can speak only with great effort when the blood flows too fast and fitfully through bodily over-exertion. Then these organs of touch are swept into the rushing current of the bloodstream and are lost in it. When, on the other hand, the blood flows too slowly, as can happen in some illnesses or in individuals who are sluggish by nature, the connection between these organs of touch and the bloodstream will not be intimate enough and, for lack of strength, speech will be wrested from the chest only with difficulty. Let us keep in mind, therefore, that downward it is the course of the blood that has a determining influence on speech.

Upward, however, the two Eustachian tubes spread out like arms and with their hand-like ends reach into the vicinity of the ear. There they hold on, grasping the ear so that hearing and speaking, address and rejoinder, can come about in immediate cooperation. In the middle ear the air organism touches the membrane of the eardrum like a hand. The membrane of the so-called circular window leading into the mysterious cavity of the inner ear is also touched. In this way the touching hand of the upper air organism is connected with the inner as well as the outer ear because, while the circular window leads into the cochlea of the ear capsule, the eardrum represents the boundary to the outer acoustic duct.

The mysterious cell where the names of things and beings are hidden is found only in the inner ear. There the eternal ideas out of which all being and becoming is formed touch the earthly realm of the human organism and pronounce their true names.

The air of the speech organism extends up to it like a hand reaching for the word inscribed in all things and beings.

The speech organism reaches above into the region of the ear and thus connects the streaming of the blood with the apprehension of names. It is in this way that the act of hearing comes about for names and words. The air organism exists not only for speaking, but also for hearing, and it intimately entwines both faculties. In the region of the mouth and nose the organs of speech have their workshop where they actively form speech. The speech organism rests on the blood, hears in the ear, and works in the mouth and nose cavities. Its centre, however, is the larynx, balancing above and below like a heart, harmonizing and uniting the tendency to fall apart or to collapse upon each other. This is only possible because the larynx is not a rigid tube but a complicated joint that is kept in continual movement by a definite number of muscles. From above and below, from front and back, muscles pass to the larynx, unite with its parts and make it into a distinct organ of the motor system. In this way speaking becomes a motor act for expression. As already emphasized in the first chapter of this book, every muscle movement calls for the participation of the entire voluntary muscular system and this holds true also for the motor nature of speech. It is completely built into the activity of the whole motor system, is part of it and cannot function without it.

Gehlen has clearly pointed to this fact. He says,

> If, with Karl Bühler, one considers 'presentation' only as one of the achievements of speech related to expression and communication, one widens the standpoint quite correctly into the sociological, but one still tends to overlook the motor side, which after all also belongs to speech. Regarded from this standpoint, speech utterances are first and foremost movements that can well be transformed into other kinds of movement. These are made use of in the education of the deaf and dumb.[3]

The whole organism of movement is characterized as the necessary foundation of all speech. This in turn presupposes an indirect inclusion of the peripheral and central nervous systems. Thus, the extremely complicated ramification of the whole process of speaking becomes evident. The organs of speech stand like a central formation within the human organism. While they are determined by it, they certainly determine it as well. The air moved in breathing is their basic substance. It touches the blood below and comes into intimate contact with the ear above. The muscular systems of larynx, throat, and mouth, as part of the complete motor apparatus, become the builders of both the substance and the form of speech.

The life of the speech organism begins at the moment of birth. The beginning has been made when the air current is drawn into the body and tone formation is accomplished with the first cry. During the embryonic period, this speech organism was at rest, being built up and formed, but at birth its activity begins, enabling the child gradually to learn speech as well as speaking.

Saying, naming, talking — three aspects

Before we describe the successive stages of acquiring speech, a few brief but fundamental explanations of terminology must be made. We pointed out in the first section of this chapter that speech itself desires to come into contact with, and to speak to, itself, that the names of things emanate from speech. Speech gives the names. We should, therefore, assign more importance to speech as a being in itself than is usually done.

We are too easily inclined to say to other people, especially if they are children, 'Think first before you speak.' But who really does this? Do we not often become aware of what we actually mean only after we have spoken? The philologist, Jespersen, repeatedly referred to the remark of the little girl who said, 'Please let me speak so that I know what I think.' How right this child was! A large part of our speaking is like a conversation we hold with our thinking. But we also converse in this way with others, and it is often this very moment of surprise at our own remarks that gives enchantment to a conversation.

I do not mean to say with this that the expression, 'I speak,' is not true. I speak, indeed, but by no means do I need to think first in order to say what I mean. In speech the ego as individuality lives not only in the realm of the waking consciousness, where thinking is accomplished, but also in the realm of dream consciousness out of which it speaks.[4]

Even as a movement becomes perceptible only after each of its parts as well as the whole have been completed, so too speech becomes fully conscious only after it has been spoken. In most cases it is true that 'I' agree with what I have said, but in cases of mistakes, and especially in pathological conditions, speech becomes a self-existent entity that often, to the horror of the speaker, seems to rise from unknown depths. Here lies one of the roots of stuttering and stammering.

'It speaks' and 'I speak,' are both true. Speech is an entity independent of me, which follows its own modalities and laws, has its own reasoning, is active by itself, and expresses itself in speaking, dwelling within me like the breath that comes and goes. It is an entity that seizes my motor organism and lifts it into the realm of the speech organs, wedding it to the air. It is an entity that also rests on the stream of my blood and reaches up to my ear. It is interwoven with me and yet is something different from what I, myself, am.

I speak the speech. That is the primary given fact, but thereby I express myself — my wishes and feelings, my hidden inclinations, my desires and my presentiments. All this is contained in the words, 'To say.' I, myself, *say* what I am by means of speech.

Speech expresses itself in speaking. This is the second function of speaking. Here speech lives in its own realm. It deciphers the eternal and temporal names of things and beings, and in this way man learns to know their names. It is not I who call things by name. In reality, I have been given speech and thus names are revealed to me. I can pronounce and also understand them. All this is contained in the words, 'To name.' Things and beings are named in the realm of speech and I am allowed to take part in it.

Speech expresses me in speaking. It lets me understand other speakers and turns me toward them. Thus, speech can come to terms with itself and with thinking. Speech is a social structure through which the wall between ego and ego can be bridged, even though often only seemingly. Conversation, talk, exchange of thoughts, all have their home here. This is expressed in the words, 'To talk.' Speech builds the bridges of talking across which I can reach the other ego.

What Karl Bühler characterizes in a primitive, one-sided way as statement, influence and presentation has its correct application here.[5] Statement is contained in saying, presentation in naming and influence in talking. Speaking encompasses all three, and speech itself is even wider and greater than speaking. Speaking is only the active side of speech, which also has a passive side — hearing. Just as speech can speak, so can it also hear the spoken word, the statement. It can hear itself in me, as well as in others insofar as they are speaking. Therefore, the tool, the speech organism, reaches up into the ear where it participates in hearing.

Thus, speech has two sides: The motor side, speaking, and the sensory side, hearing. Both must work together in unison so that speech itself can become manifest. Usually, when a child is born deaf, the child is not really deaf but his speech has not reached the sensory region. Something similar can occur in the motor area of speech. In any case, speech should be recognized as something comprehensive, embracing these two functions. At the same time, it should also be seen as something self-existent.

Schematically this can be illustrated in the following way:

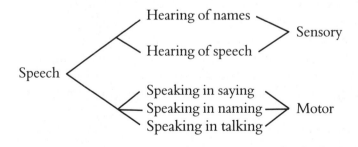

With this introduction we can go on to consider speech development as such.

The stages of speech development

How the speech organism begins to live at the moment of birth was described in the second section of this chapter. With the first breath air begins to stream in and out and the child's first cry can sound. With this event the foundation of speech is laid. As definite laws can be observed at work in acquiring the ability to stand and walk upright, so also is the gradual acquisition of speech by the young child bound to definite steps as if following a mapped-out plan.

Although the first real words are not spoken before the eleventh or twelfth months, the formation of speech actually begins with the first cry. William Stern has pointed out that the child approaches speaking in a threefold manner. First, through the expressive movements of babbling; second, through mean-ingless imitation; third, through meaningful reaction to words addressed to him. These three approaches can be distinctly observed, particularly during the first year. All three, however, are preceded by crying. The baby expresses his sensations of sympathy and antipathy in variations of crying or by making crowing sounds that the mother gradually learns to understand during the first months.

What is here called babbling in sound formation occurs only about the third month. Friedrich Kainz says the following about this babbling.

> Babbling is a functional playing of the child with his organs of articulation. Just as kicking exercises the motor apparatus, so does babbling mean an instinctive exercise and use of the muscles of the speech apparatus. It consists in the creation of articulated sound formations of syllabic and word-like character, which are at first single sounds that finally develop into endless babbling monologues ...
>
> In contrast to the sounds of crying, the products of babbling, without being true sounds of speech, gradually assume the character of speech. This becomes apparent from the fact that, besides vowels, consonants also occur.[6]

This is an apposite characterization of babbling, but it should be emphasized that it never contains word-like but only syllabic formations. All babbling consists of syllables, never of words, and rarely of single sounds. The syllable alone is the living building stone of developing word formation because the word does not consist of sounds. 'The true members of the word are rather the syllables, and the syllable comes into being through the differentiation of the breath within the stream of sound.'[7]

In babbling the baby gathers living building stones for his future words. He does so in overflowing abundance and without any sign of rationality. Although speech psychologists have tried to show in the last twenty years that the babbling of babies differs from one nation or race to another, the results have been disappointing. A French baby no more babbles in French, than does a German baby in German, or a Russian baby in Russian. Over the whole earth babies babble as if they were preparing themselves for any possible language. 'It is almost as if nature through these many-sided and unspecialized sound productions wished to create the equipment and disposition for any demands that might arise at a later date and to prepare the child for learning any possible language.'[8]

What Kainz expresses here rather professorially can be put more simply as follows. Every baby is still a citizen of the world, most certainly not of a country. With the extraordinary manifoldness of the syllables he can form, he has the possibility of learning any possible language. It is also of importance to realize that children born deaf babble to the same degree and extent as those who can hear.

Something more must be added to understand the acquisition of baby talk. The gradual preparation in the child for the understanding of everything spoken to him before the end of the first year must also be considered. Though the growing baby seems to take in the words and sentences addressed to him with increasing understanding, his comprehension does not yet constitute a word understanding in its true sense. He is given a great number of things to be perceived simultaneously, including the sounds of words and sentences. When his mother approaches and speaks a friendly word to him, when his father bends over him and lets his watch dangle in front of his nose, when one of his older brothers or sisters shows him a new toy, then the word or the spoken sentence is not of importance to him, but rather the accompanying gestures and actions, the inner approach.

One should try to feel oneself into the baby's way of experiencing. Then one will notice that he does not live in single experiences and relations to single facts, but in the totality and infinite abundance of the gradually unfolding environment. Landscapes of events open up before him with clouds of sensations, with mountains and valleys of movements and gestures, with pastures and slopes of the feelings of affection toward him. As in a landscape the sound of an animal or a human voice may be heard, so the baby hears the spoken word as part of the wholeness of his experience. He feels at first the fullness of his experience as a unity, not the word spoken in it as something separate from it. The all-embracing gesture of experience forms a first basis of understanding between him and the world, but the word is still an almost unnoticed part of this totality.

When, toward the end of the first year, the ability to stand erect occurs, when the little body raises itself from gravity and is freed from the surrounding world, then step by step he and the world grow apart. The landscape of experience begins to disintegrate into distinct parts and the child learns to feel himself separated from his surrounding world. An abyss has opened up between the without and the within.

At about this time the babbling baby talk has collected all the syllable building stones. The speech organs have come into joyful action, and the child begins to notice that the stirrings and feelings of his own world can somehow find expression in this babbling. He also has been able to acquire from the crumbling landscape of experience definite single features. Now, for example, the words, 'tick-tock,' begin to be joined with the glittering watch. The sequence of the syllables, 'Ma-ma-ma,' is attached to the appearance of his mother, but also with the longing for his mother and everything that brings comfort, satisfaction and rest.

In this manner the first true speech utterances come about in the thirteenth and fourteenth months, that is, at the beginning of the second year. At first, there was the cry and crying. Then came babbling, though neither of these two sound utterances can be called speaking. Now speaking begins, not by naming things, but rather in such a way that a single word designates a great fullness, a whole landscape of experience in which the child himself, as speaker, has become the centre. The syllable, 'Meee,' is not only the designation for milk as liquid or food, but it may also mean, 'I want milk,' or, 'I do not want milk'; 'Give me milk,' or perhaps, 'How good the milk is'; 'The milk bottle,' 'The mother who brings the milk,' or even, 'The clouds,' which sometimes are as white as milk.

This stage, which William Stern calls the stage of the one-word sentence, lasts a considerable time, terminating toward the end of the eighteenth month. During this period the child acquires between forty and seventy words, which he uses as one-word sentences.

According to what has been said in the preceding sections of this chapter, we can call this period that of 'Saying.' The child uses speech to bring himself and his strivings to expression by means of one-word sentences. It is not yet speech as such that expresses itself; the child uses speech to report about himself and his world of experience. He expresses himself in speaking.

Just as the sixth month is a decisive turning point in learning to walk when the child sits up, so in the sixth month of learning to speak, that is, in the eighteenth month, an equally decisive change occurs. Suddenly and quite spontaneously, the child grasps the connection of things through names. The child comprehends, often from one day to the next, that each thing has a name. From this moment on his vocabulary increases rapidly, so that in the course of the next six months, until about the end of the second year, four to five hundred words will have been acquired. At this time one often has the impression that words rain on the child. He catches the single drops and knows at once how to handle them, although no one has taught him how to do so.

An immediate understanding for the word itself and its meaning is present. When child psychologists say that children arbitrarily change the meaning of words in this period, they are wrong. William Stern points out, for instance, that his nineteen-month-old daughter used the name, 'nose,' for the toes of shoes.

'At this time she liked to pull our noses and discovered the same to be possible with the toes of our shoes.' But what more appropriate name than 'nose' could be used? The toes of our shoes are indeed the noses that our feet stretch out from under our skirts and trousers, thus smelling their way through the world.

To the astonishment of her father, this same daughter used the word 'doll,' not only for a real doll but also for other toys such as her stuffed rag dog and rabbit. On the other hand, she did not use the word for a little silver bell that was her favorite toy at the time. Again, nothing need astonish us here because in the child's immediate grasp of names, 'doll' is an image of man and animal. She would also use the word 'doll,' for pictures of men and animals in a book. The silver bell, however, was something totally different, and the error did not lie with the child but with the psychologist, her father, who expected the comprehensive concept, 'toy,' to be recognized by the child. For her, however, neither doll nor bell were toys, but among the various forms manifesting in an unfolding world. This can by no means be called a change of meaning in the use of words, but the meaning of words is much more comprehensive and general for the child than later on. 'Nose' is simply everything that puts a point out into the world, and 'doll' is everything that is not reality but image of reality.

For another child, 'Hooh,' can be the expression of everything connected with anxiety and surprise — darkness as well as an empty room, a mask or a veil that hides mother's face, the touch of something too cold or too warm. All this can be 'Hooh.' Because meanings are undifferentiated but immeasurably wide and intimately bound up with the world of eternal ideas, the child learns to know that each thing, anything that exists, has a name.

During this time, from the eighteenth to the twenty-fourth months, the child lives in the realm of speech that is connected with 'naming.' Everything is named and a tremendous joy fills the child during this period in which he feels himself to be a discoverer. Here is the table and there is the window; here is the moon and there are the clouds; mother, father, aunt, Liz, Bow-wow — each and everything reveals itself anew through the fact that it is named and can thus be taken into possession. Yes, the child is now not only a discoverer, but also a conqueror because what he can name belongs to him and becomes his property. At this stage, speech awakens to itself and begins to unfold in the child's soul. The child plays with speech and its words as if with the most beautiful golden balls that are thrown to him for him to possess.

During this period not only the number of words grows, but they also begin to be differentiated. Nouns, verbs and adjectives are gradually acquired and experienced according to value and meaning. The following table shows the gradual differentiation of the three categories of words during the second year.[9]

Age in years and months	Nouns	Verbs	Adjectives and Other words (except interjections)
1y 3m	100%	—	—
1y 8m	78%	22%	—
1y 11m	63%	23%	14%

This clearly shows that toward the end of the second year the child has acquired the building stones for forming the first primitive sentences. The head in the noun, the breast in the adjective and the limbs in the verb form the first basic drawing of the image of man as revealed in every simple and complex sentence. Even if the formation of the sentences is at first stiff and rigid, and the head rests too often on the earth with the limbs stretched into the air, sentence formation has nevertheless begun. The child has reached a stage in speech development similar to the one he acquired in walking when he could take the first free step in space. With sentence formation, something has been reached in the realm of speech that was experienced by the motor system in the acquisition of the ability to walk upright.

At first, the formation of sentences is clumsy, as the child lives in the period of 'naming' and therefore the names are jumbled and on top of each other. A boy may say, for instance, 'Fall stool leg Ann John,' meaning, 'John fell and bumped his leg on Ann's stool.' Gabelenz tells of a little girl who, at the age of two, climbed on a chair, fell and was smacked by her mother. She spoke of it by saying, 'Girl stool climb boom Mummy sit-upon bitten' (*Maedi Tul ketter bum mamma puch-puch bissen*). This shows clearly what can be expected in forming sentences during the period of naming. Everything is name, the being as well as the thing, the experience as well as the sensation springing from it.

When the threshold of the second year has been crossed, true sentence formation gradually begins. If previously all words have been names, they now become nouns, verbs and adjectives. In astonishment, William Stern expresses what holds true for this period:

> What effort has to be expended later on at school in learning a second language, which is never really mastered even after many years of practice! On the other hand, the speech of his environment seems to flash upon the normal child of two or three years of age. Without ever learning vocabulary or studying grammar he makes the most astounding progress month after month.[10]

This observation is certainly correct. The occurrence that Stern describes, however, cannot be really understood until one comes to realize that it is not the child who learns the language, but the language itself that unfolds within the child's speech organism.

Kainz has the following to say on this matter. 'At first the child becomes aware of the fact that in the number of words at his disposal a great variety is contained — designations for persons and things, happenings and conditions, qualities, actions, etc.'[11] On no account, however, can one say that it is the child who becomes aware of these facts and makes the relevant differentiations. Anyone who has ever observed children at the age of two or two and a half years old knows that such an assumption is nonsense. It is not the child himself but the language that begins to unfold and to express itself in speech. In the child the urge arises to tell and this urge awakens speech, which now reaches the point we called 'talking' in Section 3 of this chapter. Speech speaks the child. It hears what sounds from without and surrenders to what the urge of the child demands. One's native language is arising.

One's native language unfolds astonishingly quickly in the course of the third year. The sentences, at first so stiff and totally inarticulate, gradually begin to take shape and to assume form and life. Just as when, in the wake of the first steps, the manifold possibilities of upright mobility are acquired only gradually, and the child must learn through weeks and months of practice to come from walking to running, skipping, jumping, turning and dancing in order truly to conquer space, so also in speaking something similar is happening.

Words begin to develop, to be inflected and changed. A noun is gradually differentiated into singular and plural, and transformed by use of the several cases. The verb, as a word designating time, acquires character from the experience of past, present and future. The adjectives begin to indicate comparison, and prepositions and articles come into use. One sees how the shapeless, jointed doll brought about by the first attempts at sentence formation is imbued with life and soul, stretches and expands, and soon begins to walk and skip. Thus 'talking' comes into being.

Only in talking is the true acquisition of one's native language accomplished, and this is possible only because the child grows up in a speaking environment. Speech speaks with the other speakers and expresses the personality of the child. Speech assumes a social character and the child grows into a language community, that is, into the community of his people.

The babbling baby was a world citizen. Through the stages of saying, naming and talking he becomes a citizen of his country because he has acquired his native language. Through this he again takes possession of the world, which at first he had to push away from himself. It was through the acquisition of uprightness that the separation came about between world and self, but now through the gift of speech the self as person reconquers the world. All that we can name becomes our property, for we learn to possess it when its name is revealed to us.

The small child now resembles Noah, who gathers around him in the Ark the world belonging to him. The sons and daughters and all animals that he himself calls by name, are now his own. Outside is the flood, the waters rise, yet the safety of the Ark gives protection and confidence. That is the situation in which the child finds himself when he is about two years old. Soon Noah will release the dove in order to learn whether or not the flood has subsided. So the child will send out the doves of his first thoughts as soon as he has acquired the security of speaking.

Learning one's native language

Now that the stages of saying, naming and talking in the acquisition of speech have been described, it is easy to see that these three activities are fitted in the most intimate way into what was outlined as the speech organism in Section 2 of this chapter. This, though a unit, still shows a threefold form. It reaches below to the region of the lungs where the blood opens itself to the air. Above, it comes in direct contact with the realm of the ear through the Eustachian tubes, and in the centre where the larynx and the organs of the mouth are at work, it surrenders to the in and out streaming air. The threefoldness of speech corresponds to this anatomical-physiological threefoldness.

From below, where blood and air meet, and where the motor organism rises, 'saying' ascends. It leads the desires and wishes, the strivings and personal emotions into the realm of speech to give them expression. Here lies hidden a separate world of speech, which uses the one-word sentence far beyond the age of childhood. When we make demands, give orders, or use angry or abusive language, but also when we want something with longing or impatience, it is the sphere of saying that brings this to expression. Whether I yell, 'Scoundrel!' to one, or 'Hey, waiter!' to another, these are one-word sentences that according to my emphasis expresses what I mean. Saying breaks forth from below and goes upward.

From above downward, however, from the ear to the larynx, 'naming' flows and streams. Where the sphere of hearing becomes the source of a special sense, called by Rudolf Steiner the sense of speech, the names of things have their own world. There speech learns the names and they stream into the region of the larynx and express themselves in speaking. Anything we can name with words has its realm here. Whether they are men or animals, things or plants, concrete or abstract, we grasp them all through names. Naming streams toward saying from above downward and unites and mixes with it, although it exists in itself. Naming streams down from the ear to the larynx.

'Talking,' on the other hand, is born in the streaming in and out of the air in breathing. Therefore, it is the social element in the realm of speech. It weaves between man and man, between speaker and speaker. It carries the play of question and answer from soul to soul. Naming streams into us from above, saying mingles with it from below, and thus speaking itself, or talking, appears at the end as if it were a unity. Talking, however, is also an independent element itself and lives in the outward flow of the stream of our breath.

Syllables build the saying. Words form the elements of naming. The sentence becomes the garment of talking. In this way syllables, words and sentences also receive their domain, and here the infinitely complex and manifold ties linking speech and speaking to man become apparent. In the previously mentioned lecture on spiritual science and speech Rudolf Steiner describes the mystery of speech with these words:

> The development of speech is, indeed, only comparable to artistic activity. We cannot demand that speech shall be an exact copy of what it intends to present any more than we can demand that the artist's imitation shall correspond to reality. Speech reproduces only the external, in the sense in which the artist's picture reproduces it. Before man was a self-conscious spirit in the modern sense, an artist, working as the spirit of speech, was active ... It is a subconscious activity that has produced the speaking human being as a work of art. By analogy speech must be conceived as a work of art ...[12]

These words reveal that speech is the work of the spirit of speech, who once created it in man. It is a work of art and if we try to comprehend it artistically, we recognize the three members of which we have spoken.

Speech pathology from stammering to dumbness, from word blindness to sensory and motor aphasia will only be seen in the right way if 'saying,' 'naming' and 'talking' are recognized in their specific characteristics. The manifoldness of these abnormalities can only be understood as the falling apart of this threefoldness, which must become a unity in speaking if speech is to express itself, and as the inharmonious working together of these three members and the inability to weld them together or keep them apart. This is intended merely as an indication because a more detailed treatment of the subject would go beyond the scope of this book.

Whenever one has to deal with speech, its extent, magnitude and dimension seem so vast that it is impossible to do justice to what in truth is an eternal being. Therefore, I close this chapter with the words that Hamann, the wise man from the north, expressed in his book, *The Last Will and Testament of the Knight of the Rosy Cross*:

> Every phenomenon of nature was a word — the sign,
> symbol and pledge of a new, secret, unspeakable but all
> the more intimate union, communication and
> community of design, energies and ideas. All that man in
> the beginning heard, saw with his eyes, beheld and what
> he touched with his hands was a living word; for God
> was the Word. With this Word in mouth and heart the
> origin of speech was as natural, as near and as easy as
> child's play ...[13]

Chapter 3

The Awakening of Thinking

Prerequisites for the awakening of thinking

The third year, which we shall now take into consideration, is of decisive importance for the further development of the child. In the first year he detached himself from the world by the acquisition of the ability to walk upright, and learned to distinguish between the experience of the surrounding world and his own existence. In the second year, through the birth of speech, the things of the surrounding world were named and the manifoldness of speaking, especially in saying and naming, for the first time brought order into the bewildering diversity of life experience. The outer as well as the inner world could now be threaded somehow on the string of words and primitive sentences and could be used for his adornment like the colourful little chains that the child produced at this time. The small child looked at himself with greatest pleasure in the mirror of his own word power and wore the speech he had acquired like a festive garment. This garment was a house that offered shelter and gave security. Whenever the garment had a hole, when a word or sentence construction was missing or not altogether successful, disappointment pierced the child's soul. Indeed, it may even have led to despair.

In the third year, the time lasting from the extended acquisition of speech to the appearance of the first period of defiance, an entirely new event occurs — thinking begins to awaken. This happens in quite special moments, often lifted out of everyday life, during which the child begins to become conscious of himself as personality. These moments may appear only seldom and grow more frequent and decisive only in later years. During the third year, however, they begin to be seen. Then the child becomes a being who observes himself and the world no longer as a child but as a person conscious of his own self.

Many conditions are necessary for this awakening to occur. Some of these are more important than others, but a diversity of these acquired prerequisites is necessary. I shall mention only the most essential ones that will occupy us further. Firstly, the elaboration of speech must be considered because children begin to learn the correct formation of sentences only at the end of the second year when the word as such becomes a phenomenon that livingly changes and transforms itself. Comparison of adjectives, declension of nouns, and tenses of verbs are gradually achieved. In this way the experience of time and space is multiplied and recognition of the things themselves is considerably broadened.

Secondly, the acquisition of memory is an indispensable basis for the awakening of thinking. To this belongs the gradual formation of memories from vague recognition to voluntary reproduction of memory ideas.

A third requirement is play. Here the free activity of the small child as expressed in every new forms of play, in the imitation of the world of grown-ups, and in the enlivening of his own fantasy is of fundamental importance. How else would a child be able to recognize himself as a person if he did not repeat, imitate, and, as a non-ego, put in front of himself everything he sees happening around him? The true meaning of all play is that the child creates the world in play in such a way that he himself does not take part in his creation because he is the creator. As such he can withdraw from what he has created.

A fourth requirement is the gradual comprehension of an idea of time encompassing first the future and later the past. There must also be a gradually developing comprehension of space where one cannot only walk and run, but where individual things are kept such as toys in the toy-chest and clothes in the closet. Houses and lanes, fields and paths with their trees and shrubs also become well-known sights. Another thing to consider in understanding certain attitudes of the child is that the smaller the child the larger he experiences himself in relation to the world of space.

Finally, we must take note of how percepts are gradually grasped and transformed into ideas, a process intimately connected with the formation of memory, which will be mentioned later.

With all these single soul functions, which in the course of his third year the child not only acquires but also develops and connects with each other, we have some notion of the complexity of these developments. What we call the 'awakening of thinking' can only arise in this manifoldness and working together. Speech and ideas, memory and play, the comprehension of space and time are like a circle of kind women who bend over the cradle in which a sleeping child is on the point of waking up. Each of the women makes a helping gesture and calls an encouraging word to the child, who is the 'thinking' about which we shall speak. Thus, the process of awakening comes about.

We must next try to describe what this awakening thinking is not and what it is. Only after we have reached an understanding on this point can something be said in clarification of the third year in the life of a child.

What human thinking is not, and what it is

First, we must clear away the nonsense of the views that began with Köhler's *Investigation of Anthropoid Apes*.[1] These views were introduced into child psychology by Karl Bühler[2] and have since spread from his work like a malignant growth (for example, Remplein[3]). I refer to Köhler's well-known and instructive experiments on a number of anthropoid apes. Here he tried to show that the results he obtained were primitive achievements of intelligence. For instance, some of the chimpanzees, after unsuccessful attempts, were able to reach fruit that was hung from the ceiling, by piling boxes on top of each other. In another experiment the 'more intelligent' of the animals learned to put together previously prepared sticks so as to reach fruit lying outside their cage. Several other ingenious methods were used by Köhler to arrive at these so-called achievements of intelligence.

Bühler, as an experimental psychologist, was lured by these experiments into subjecting children eight to sixteen months of age to similar situations. For instance, he put a pane of glass between the hands of a child and a biscuit the child wanted in order to test how and when the child would summon the 'intelligence' to reach around the glass for the delicacy. But the child usually failed him. In another experiment, a piece of bread attached to a thread was put in front of the child in such a way that he could reach the thread but not the bread. The child was then supposed to pull the food toward him by means of the thread. The results of these experiments caused Bühler to say in all seriousness, 'Indeed, there is a phase in the life of a child that one might well designate the chimpanzee age. In the case of this particular child it was about the tenth, eleventh or twelfth month.'

A person can accept or reject this as he pleases. The idea, however, that a ten-month-old child, in the environment of his home, hardly yet able to move, should be compared with grown-up chimpanzees in their cages is possible only with the kind of thinking prevalent at the beginning of the twentieth century. Furthermore, the word intelligence is thoroughly abused here. This animal behaviour — and that is what was meant here — is by no means an achievement of thinking. When placing one box on top of the other, or putting sticks together, the chimpanzees are not intellectually putting two and two together, but their desire for the fruit dictates the movements of their limbs in such a way that they use the objects lying about to satisfy this desire.

It would be an accomplishment of real intelligence only if a chimpanzee would break a branch from a tree and prepare it to use as a fetching stick. Or, again, if he could make a box out of boards by using smaller and harder pieces of wood as nails and a stone as a hammer in order then to put the box to a use thought out in advance. But nothing of the kind happens in Köhler's experiments in which well-prepared objects are so placed that instinct and desire can make use of them. What happens is nothing more than the bringing together of parts, perceived by the senses, into meaningful order through the power of desire. Nothing like this is meant when we speak here of the awakening of thinking.

W. Stern once called 'intelligence' that faculty 'which adjusts itself to new demands by orderly disposition of the means of thought.'[4] Stern speaks of means of thought that are the basis of an intelligent achievement. These, however, are present neither in the chimpanzee nor in the one-year old child, as Köhler or Bühler try to understand them.

The foundations necessary for the awakening of thinking are laid only as speech begins to develop in the child. Speech is like a plough that works the field of the soul so that the seed of future thought achievement can be laid into the open furrows. Even seemingly sensible utterances of the child cannot be interpreted as thought achievement. If, for instance, he begins to name things and then not only recognizes but also designates them upon seeing them repeatedly, this is by no means an act of thought but only of memory within the framework of speech.

Also, when the child begins to identify what he has drawn, painted or otherwise copied, for example, a picture of a cat with the actual object and then calls it by its correct name, even this behaviour cannot be ascribed to the acquisition of thought. While certainly complex, this is almost entirely an act of memory as function of recognition.

It has already been mentioned that memory, like speech, is necessary for the preparation of thinking. The seeds that are sown into the furrows of the field of speech are those pictures and names, ideas and sensations that memory retains for the small child. It is the result of the power of memory that the acquisition of these pictures does not continually dissolve and vanish. Memory alone preserves in the child's soul the names of things in their connection with the arising imagery. Out of these seeds grow the first few green blades of true thinking in the course of the third year.

What do we call this thinking? In his third year, for example, a child has great difficulties in acquiring an idea of space or time. He can ask, 'Is today tomorrow?' or, 'Is yesterday today?' W. Stern tells how one of his children said, 'When we travel home, it is today.' Or again, 'We want to pack today and travel yesterday.' Something here endeavors to bring into a correct order yesterday, today and tomorrow so that something that exists, though not perceptible, touchable or audible, still receives its rightful place. The child already knows in his feeling that there is a 'has been' and a 'to come.' That lives in him as a dim feeling. That today may become tomorrow's yesterday, however, emerges only gradually as thought structure from the experience of manifold world happenings. It is these invisible, but thinkable structures inscribed into the experienced reality that the child begins to grasp.

If, one day, he begins to ponder during a meal and says, 'Daddy spoon, Mummy spoon, Auntie spoon, Bobby spoon, all spoon!' he has truly made the tremendous discovery that there are objects of the same order. He has come to know that not every single thing has its own name but a number of the same things have a common name, that all spoons are called 'spoon' and that everybody — Daddy, Mummy, Auntie and child — possesses a spoon. The great moment has come when thinking begins to awaken to a conscious function. The first acts of thinking do not occur before this time, but after this they continue to increase as the child grows older, until at school age they become regular, daily activities.

We should not, as still happens today, mistake purposeful soul activities that will lead to ordered actions for true acts of thinking. Even the unconscious accomplishes many of the actions it quite reasonably strives for. Animals often show in their behaviour unimaginably clear and concrete reasoning. Indeed, reasonable behaviour is evident in the way bees build their combs, ants prepare their food, wasps safeguard the future of their brood. Hundreds of such examples could be given. This kind of reasoning, however, works out of the organic realm and does not comprehend itself. As active intelligence it only uses organisms as tools.

In contrast, the thinking of the child, when it awakens in the third year, is reason that comprehends and becomes conscious of itself. That power lying hidden in all things, which orders, works and shapes, now arises in the human head as body-free activity and grows into awakening thought. This even occurs for the first time in the course of the third year. It will occupy us in detail in later sections of this chapter. First, however, the pre-requisites that lead to the activity of thinking must be studied.

Speech as the first prerequisite for thought

After the child has learned 'saying' and 'naming' in the course of his second year and has tried to express himself in somewhat wooden sentence fragments, the whole realm of speech begins to quicken in the third year. As we have already mentioned, we can actually experience how the helpless jointed doll of the first attempts at sentences is gradually permeated with life and soul, stretches and expands and soon begins to walk and to hop.

What the child now acquires is the living incorporation of what he later has to learn intellectually as grammar. Especially the morphology of words and the art of forming sentences, or syntax, begin to awaken in him. Language gives birth to itself in all its perfect grandeur and beauty. Now declination, conjugation and comparison are learned, not, however, in the way they will be learned later, but in such a way that, through the imitation and agility of the child, the words themselves unfold their own life. The endless possibilities of description for everything offered the child by the variety of his experiences thus arise. Merely in the fact that he begins to use nouns, verbs and adjectives, the world opens up to him as being in existence (noun), is constantly active in doing and suffering (verb), and is also subject to judgment and description by others (adjective). Thus noun, verb and adjective form the archetypal picture not only of all sentence formation, but of all manner of manifestations of earth existence.

With the beginning of the declension of nouns* comes the child's first sensations for the way things and beings appear and are related to each other: In the nominative still isolated, limited and related to itself; in the genitive describing ownership, membership, partnership; in the dative referring to the quality, the place, the time and grasping the thing or being as object; in the

---

* This book was originally written in German where nouns have four cases and one of three genders.

accusative describing more the quantity, representing the spatial expanse and the length of time.[5]

The differentiation between singular and plural, and between masculine, feminine and neuter begins to emerge. Something like the theory of categories as they were first discovered and described by Aristotle becomes alive in the speaking child. In speaking, the child repeats on the level of the word all relations of things and beings of the surrounding world. When even the verb with its conjugations gradually becomes the child's property — as transitive, intransitive or reflexive, indicating whether it is a case of general activity (to blossom, to think, to fall) (or relating to a person or thing — then a feeling for the manifoldness of all that happens arises in the child. When through conjunctions the activity of the event is so described that it can be represented according to person, number, time, manner and condition, the application of this theory of categories is extended almost without limit.

The child begins to speak about past and future and thus concepts of time are evolved that lead later to a past perfect and imperfect or conditional, and to a picture of the conditional. Lastly, the growing human being learns to define himself more and more as a subject acting in the present.

In the adjective the child learns to point to single characteristics and to ascribe to a thing consisting of many relations and qualities, one definite characteristic that he singles out. These single indications are also discovered in other things and compared with the quality comprehended first. In this way comparison is gradually developed. That this does not come about easily is demonstrated by the study of the child, Annie,[6] who, when shown the drawings of three towers of unequal size at the age of two and a half years, said that one of them was large, the other small and the middle one thick. The comprehension of a comparable ratio of size did not yet exist. For some time this comparison seemed to Annie the only possible one because the comprehension of the comparison of three similar things was only formed toward the end of the third year.

An endless number of examples could be cited to demonstrate gradual maturing in the comprehension of a living grammar. The child is also much more mobile than the adult in declension and conjugation and uses words with an overflow of formative power. He will not say, 'The sheep,' but, 'The sheeps,' not, 'The feet,' but, 'The foots,' in order to mark the difference between singular and plural in the form of the word.

But these are all only a preparation for thinking, not yet the act of thinking itself. They are the numberless furrows and figures that the plough of speech imprints into the field of the soul. Rudolf Steiner once pointed out the fundamental difference between thought and speech when he said, 'Human thinking takes place to a large extent consciously. Speech is not conscious in the same degree. A person needs little self-consciousness to realize that he does not speak with the same degree of consciousness with which he thinks.'[7] In this half-consciousness, which does not lie as deep as dream-consciousness, but unfolds in the region between dreaming and waking, the child learns to speak.

When a child produces new designations for things he cannot yet name, when he produces names that are either entirely new creations or combinations or transformation of otherwise known words, it is not the child's thinking, but rather the innate formative force of language that performs this and expresses itself through the child. When, therefore, Annie was asked the name of her clown (Punch), she first said, 'Rinka,' then 'Rinkus,' then 'Pasta.' She produced a kind of word salad in her joy of creating new words. E. Köhler had observed correctly when she added, 'I believe Annie would be able when in full swing, to improvise another half dozen new words.'[8] The same child called skimmed milk, 'water-milk,' a rubble heap, 'dirt mountain,' a mortar, 'sugar rammer,' or 'sugar stamper,' and the railway conductor, 'Mr Railway Station,' explaining, 'the man in the train ... who pinches the cards.' But this is not the case of an explanation of a thoughtlike nature, but a description and combination of sense and speech experience.

These examples show the tremendous plastic power that lives in the child's language. This calls to mind an indication of Rudolf Steiner:

Man would not have spoken at that time (before the Fall) as he does today, for speech had not as yet been differentiated into languages. This differentiation came about because speech had become somewhat fixed. ... There was no such thing as a fixed language in that far-off time of which we are speaking, but each object, each impression, was instantly responded to by a gesture, a tone gesture from within man. By means of speech man entered completely into any being that approached him from without. Speech in its later development was but a degenerate earthly result, the fallen remnant of that original, light-filled language ...[9]

A trace of this originally intended state reappears in the child's ever recurring new word creations.

Through the totality of grammar the 'fallen remnant' of language carries within it as image the reasoning of the whole universe. Of this Steiner speaks at length and shows how living forces of reason permeate single words, so that the French word, 'courage,' for instance, combines the words, 'coeur' and 'rage' and thus points to the life and enthusiasm radiating from the heart. That is how reason would describe the word, 'courage.' 'These are not just inventions,' said Steiner. 'They are real events that truly happened. Thus are words formed.'[10]

We now come to the first understanding of that mighty foundation that the world of speech gives to the child for the development of his thinking. In the realm of speech as a whole there lives an all-wielding reason in which the child takes part when he speaks. He cannot yet think alone and independently, but in speaking, he practices the rules of reason, for grammar is the logic of language, a universal logic that later will be raised to the individual logic of the thinking person.

Memory

The second sphere into which the child has to grow in the third year is the realm of remembrance and memory. In the course of the third year the development of the faculty of memory receives a decisive impetus and assumes its rightful place. At the end of the third year memory has been so far perfected that it has become a fundamental part of the experience of consciousness. From this time on the thread of memories develops and soon becomes a continuum for daily experiences.

Though this development of memory is of great importance for the awakening of thought, these two soul activities are fundamentally different. The development of memory in the small child poses many problems. In basic outline, however, the development of memory is open to study nowadays, especially on the basis of what Rudolf Steiner has to say. He once described how, in the development of human history a threefold transformation of the faculty of memory has taken place. In primeval times of Atlantean development it began with the formation of a localized memory.

> If, in that time of which I have spoken, one were to enter the region inhabited by people who were still conscious of their head, chest, heart and limbs, one would see on every hand small pegs placed in the earth and marked with a sign, or here and there a sign made upon a wall. Such memorials were to be found scattered over all inhabited regions. Wherever anything happened, a man would set up some kind of memorial, and when he came back to the place, would relive the event in the memorial he had made.[11]

This localized memory was followed by rhythmical memory.

> Man felt a need to reproduce within himself what he heard in such a way that rhythm was formed. If his experience of a cow, for instance, suggested, 'moo,' he did not simply call her, 'moo,' but 'moo-moo,' and perhaps in ancient times, 'moo-moo-moo.' That is to say his perception was as it were piled up to produced a rhythm.'

Rudolf Steiner calls the third form of memory, 'time memory.'

> What is quite matter of fact for us in the wretched abstractness of modern man first appeared then — a time

memory, in which we produce something as a picture
and no longer have the experience of having had to recall
something that was to be brought up again by awakening
it in rhythmic repetition and in unconscious or semi-
conscious activity.[12]

At the transition from the Atlantean to the post-Atlantean cul-
tural epoch around the year 8000 BC, the change from localized
to rhythmical memory took place. When the high cultures of
Asia Minor were succeeded by that of Greece, at about the time
of the Trojan War and the laying of the foundation stone of
Europe, rhythmical memory changed into picture memories.

It is quite obvious that localized memory is established
through our limbs by erecting markers in our surroundings.
Our hands build primitive and simple memorials. Rhythmical
memory utilizes the element of speech and song. Finally, picture
or time memory pertains to the head. Accordingly, these three
forms of memory ascent and wander from the movement of the
limbs up to the resting head via the motor activity of speech.

It is significant that there still exist in German language
words exactly indicating these memory forms. There is the
word, *merken* (to remember), which we still have in *marke*,
markierung, *markstein* (mark, marking, landmark). I mark something in the sense of 'mark my word' by making a remark about
it to myself or finding a landmark outside for it. The second
word is *besinnen*, which comes from *sinnen* (to meditate, ponder,
think, to be minded). The sound already contains a rhythmical
element, which may turn from the inward *sinnen* to the outward
singing. Songs and sagas, those rhythmically recited epics calling
up in the listener the rhythmical memory, belong here. From
the *Bhagavad Gita* to the Songs of Homer and the *Nibelungenlied*,
they formed and fashioned rhythmical memory. The third word
is *Erinnern* (re-member, re-collect). What was laid into the
innermost soul now reascends as *er-innerung* (re-collection).[13]
This is the form of memory that prevails today and that we all
know.

Thus we can draw up the following table to indicate the
totality of memory.

	First step:	Localized remembering = 'marking.'
Memory ←	Second step:	Rhythmic remembering = 'be-thinking.'
	Third step:	Picture remembering = 'recollecting.'

These stages of memory are strikingly featured in the development of the small child's memory. Karl Bühler has an inkling of this when he says,

> It is a fact that what we differentiated abstractly as a path from below upward through steps or phases, the child passes through in the development of his memory activity in all reality. This means that we can discover first vague impressions of familiarity ... then the experiences of more definite recognition and finally complete memories ordered according to space, time and logic.'[14]

Bühler describes indistinctly what appears clearly in the threefoldness of memory as outlined by Rudolf Steiner.

During his first year the child is filled almost entirely with a localized memory. He experiences the impressions of familiarity, described by Bühler, when his mother's face appears again and again, when his little sister bends over the side of the crib, when light and darkness approach him alternately. Here 'landmarks' appear from outside and vaguely fashion the basis of 'marking' (*merken*).

In the second year when speech develops, rhythmic memory begins to be formed. Newly learned words are now said over and over again to exhaustion, and new forms of movement are continually repeated. A picture book is repeatedly brought out and looked at as the acquired sounds are uttered. During this second year the child seems possessed by rhythm and everything he does is repeated. Moreover, the localized memory expands. Certain places are sought out with pleasure, others avoided with trepidation because certain memories are connected with them. At the same time the beginnings of the third form of memory appear.

These first traces of memory ideas (*Erinnerungsvorstellungen*),
even if only fleeting, appear from the second year onward.
Around the middle of the second year, however,
memories of longer duration also begin to emerge. Here
the twenty-four hour period has a preferential position (in
the order of periodicity).

Thus it is described by Stern[15] who is justified in pointing to the
periodicity because the picture memories are still shadows over
against the lively experiences of the rhythmic memories.

When a two-year-old child demands that the same thing
should happen every day at the same time, or that a fairy tale
must be repeated with the same expressions and accents of feeling, it is indicative of the rhythmic memory that governs this age.

Toward the end of the third year memory ideas become
more frequent and insert themselves widely into the totality of
memories. The ability to 'mark' (*merkfähigkeit*) and 'be-think'
(*besinnung*) are gradually overpowered by the third form of
memory.

The child now learns to remember what has been imparted
by means of speech and he becomes receptive to teaching and
admonition. These acquisitions are already the result of the
awakening thinking. More will be said about this later.

At this time the child acquires the first picture of his past,
because the power of reflection begins to unfold in his soul. W.
Stern describes it in an impressive way:

We have already had to emphasize in several places the
slight acquaintance between the little child and his past. It
is true that he owes all his knowledge and his capabilities
to his past and its after-effects, but he is not yet able to
look back to it ... In the mist that hides the child's past
from his consciousness, faint, indistinct and fleeting
points of light appear here and there. They grow plainer,
more varied and frequent with increasing years and later
combine in somewhat greater numbers ... Many years
pass, however, before these separate parts unite and form
a whole, giving the child a connected picture ...[16]

In this way, toward the end of the third year, the memory frame for the experience of personality is formed. The child, whose past gradually begins to emerge, is far enough along to gain an idea of his personality. This is at first only a dull sensation, but in contrast to the situation of the smaller child, it exists. Closed forms of his existence light up in him only in his recognition of things and situations, or in the rhythmic repetition of actions including speaking.

Thus the acquisition of memory becomes one of the most important prerequisites for the child's experience of his own person.

Fantasy and play

In connection with the appearance of picture memory, which is in effect a result of the forming of ideas, fantasy, another soul power, grows in the child. Rudolf Steiner has shown the polarity that exists between memory and fantasy or imagination. He says, 'Just as pictorial thinking is based upon antipathy, willing is based upon sympathy. If sympathy is strong enough, as when thoughts become memory through antipathy, then imagination is created through sympathy.'[17] Presented schematically these connections can be seen more distinctly:

Knowledge	Will
Antipathy	Sympathy
Memory	Fantasy

W. Stern, at the beginning of his chapter on play and fantasy indicated the significance of fantasy when he wrote, 'Where shall we begin and where end? The material available is nowhere so overwhelming as in the consideration of fantasy and play.'[18] Fantasy is one of the strongest characteristics of infancy, but it also has a special position that is not always clearly recognized. One is too readily inclined to derive the power of fantasy from the child's ordinary life of ideas. Even Stern does not get beyond this prejudice. He says, 'The concrete image of the fantasy-percept is not, however, the direct production of outer impressions, but the result of inner working.... The percept (*Vorstellung*) is experienced independently and enjoyed as his own creation."*

One does not attain a true view of those forces underlying fantasy with this interpretation because fantasy takes hold of any kind of material, movements as well as ideas, for activating itself. Any of these materials is the plastic substance used by fantasy. When the child grasps a stick and makes out of it a horse, a hat, an arrow and then a doll in quick succession, what he has done has little to do with the stick itself. Or if he takes an idea and with its help makes himself a soldier, a father or a conductor, this action also has little in common with the idea. Fantasy seizes anything it can get hold of. Only be recognizing the intimate interweaving between play and fantasy can we do justice to fantasy because fantasy without play, and play without fantasy are almost unthinkable. Even when the child begins to make up stories at bedtime, this, too, is play, a play of fantasy with the ideas of memory.

Here we have two pairs of contrasts that we must consider. Just as fantasy is bound up with playing, so does memory work in close union with speaking. The faculty of memory is most intimately connected with the faculty of naming because one truly remembers only what is to be named. The memory picture in turn is developed with the name. Play, on the other hand, enlivens fantasy; conversely, fantasy kindles and diversifies play.

When Stern says,[19] 'Fantasy is never able to create out of nothing. Its elements must always have their foundation in real experiences,' one has to reply that in reality it seems to be exactly the other way around. Real experiences have their sources only in the child's fantasy. After all, the child can grasp his environment only as interpretation of his fantasy, and existence gains its true meaning and becomes experience in this way alone. Fantasy is the continuous joy that the child experiences on his waking to the earthly world. His inclination toward all things and beings, his joyful urge to take everything in, to connect things with each other, to mix, to enhance is fantasy, and its expression is play.

---

* In the context of this book, the translators would have chosen the word, idea, instead of percept.

Memory on the other hand is the result of the child's painful collision with the world. The experience of the surrounding world as something alien, something veiled and impenetrable, gives the child the power of memory. In memory he can abstract the world, a process similar to what happens in the formation of words, and the world thereby becomes property, albeit a painful and abstract property.

When we see a foal jump in the meadow, we directly experience the fanciful (fantasy-filled) play of the animal. It is pleased with itself in the joy of existence, in the happiness of being part of the world. Its power of fantasy makes it skip and gallop, neigh and shake, and what is so charmingly revealed here for such a short span of time in the animals, becomes apparent in the child over many years and in manifold ways. The continuous joy of existence and uniting ever anew with the world around, this dawning and all-embracing sympathy is the origin of all fantasy.

Like all play, fantasy, too, has its well-spring in motor activity. The small child takes his fantasy from movement and mobility, from his ceaseless need for lively activity. When he moves his arms, each movement becomes a corresponding picture. When he runs or skips, jumps or climbs, immediately and naturally each of these forms of movement is embedded in a story that often begins or ends in fragments, begins without ending, and ends without having begun. But that is the fascination of all play, that there is no beginning and no ending, and yet all is happening.

Only later, when movement is performed without a picture behind it, when movement is done for movement's sake, when it has become purpose in itself, will the abstraction of sport have been attained.

When, toward the end of the second year, motor activity has freed itself, fantasy begins to arise and gradually take form in the course of the third year. From then on it is preserved during most of childhood and is forced down into the subconscious only at prepuberty by thinking that forms ideas, and memories that advance with ever-increasing strength into the foreground.

One of the first to do justice to fantasy was Ernst Feuchtersleben. He devoted a whole chapter to it in his *Diaetetik der Seele*, where he said, 'Fantasy is the bread winner, the prime mover of all single members of the spiritual organism. Without it all ideas stagnate, however great their number. Concepts remain rigid and dead, sensations raw and sensuous ... One can say fantasy is in us before we ourselves are, and it remains until we have gone.' These words point to the all-embracing power of fantasy, which beyond childhood comes into the foreground of the soul only when it is withdrawn from waking consciousness and is enwrapped in the dreams of narcotic confusion of memory and thought.

So we see in the third year a period during which the child makes a threefold acquisition. With the powers of his head he gradually comes into possession of memory in the form of ideas. With his middle organization he gains quickening speech, learns to form sentences and begins to hold real conversations; talking is acquired. Finally, fantasy, born out of his limb system, comes to full blossom in the child. This threefold acquisition is the necessary preparatory step for the beginning of the activity of thinking proper in its first tender form. The highest gift bestowed upon the growing human being — his cognition, his ability to know — is developed in the soul realm of remembering, speaking and fantasy. In this process of the awakening of thought he becomes conscious of himself and the word 'I' as self-designation, is formed at the same time. 'I think' becomes at first a rare experience whose recurrence gradually increases.

The earliest achievements in thinking

E. Köhler describes Annie's first attempts at thinking at the age of two years and six months in the following way:

> When there is something that Annie does not fully understand, she ponders, stands quietly and puts her hands behind her back; her eyes grow large and gaze into the distance; her mouth contracts a little and she is silent; after this exertion she gets a little tired; the expression vanishes; nature arranges for relaxation.[20]

Awakening thought reveals itself here in its outer gesture. The child withdraws from the world of sense impressions and overcomes her impulse to move, assuming a position similar to that of listening. She begins to listen to her awakening thoughts.

These first, softly sounding thoughts contain the dawn of an understanding for the fact that the world of things and beings show mysterious relationships, that here and there, at different places the same thing can happen and that tomorrow and today similar events can take place; that definite objects perform functions appropriate to them and that every human being stands in similar connections to other human beings.

Thus, Annie had learned in her second year to call her father, Daddy, and all other men, Uncle. Before that, all men had been Daddy, her Daddy. But at the end of the third year when she saw a young man leading a dog, she said, 'Look, the dog goes for a walk with his Daddy.' She had grasped the connection child-father and this is shown soon afterward when she called an uncle with whose son she was playing, 'The other Daddy.'

At about the same time Annie plays a question game with her father. In answer to the question, 'Who makes the dress?' he says, 'The dressmaker.' Annie perseveres and then asks, 'Who makes the apron?' At the same moment she remembers that the apron she is wearing was sewn by her mother. The father, who knows nothing of this, answers, 'The dressmaker.' Annie, however, interrupts and says, 'No, Mummy! Mummy is a dressmaker.' With this the child has discovered an activity that is not only that of the dressmaker, but also that of her mother. The identification of an activity has resulted and her world has become richer by a new connection.

Such identifications start in the course of the third year and are at first simple, becoming more complicated and manifold later on. The same Annie at the age of two years and five months was given a doll named Tony. One day her Aunt drew a picture of Tony on a piece of paper. The child got quite excited because she recognized the identity and yet sensed that the drawing was something different from the object itself. After she had then found and brought Tony to her aunt, she was asked about the meaning of the drawing. She explained, 'A dolly ... like that!' The moment this is grasped, the tension dissolves. Object and image are recognized!

By means of speech a child finds his first access to another thought achievement, which along with identification is of greatest importance: The relationship expressed by 'when ... then,' 'because,' or 'for'; the fact that one thing happens when or because another thing happens. The first primitive formation of subordinate clauses helps the child to take a big step forward. Stern calls this the fourth speech stage and says:

> Like inflexion, hypotaxis (the subordination of one sentence to another) is a form of speech completely wanting in many languages that can express the dependency relationship of thoughts only by putting sentences side by side (parataxis). The child of a European civilization passes this stage in about two and a half years and proves that he has grasped not only the logical connection of thoughts but also their value relationship as represented in principal and subordinate clauses.[21]

Little Hilde Stern could already manage the following formulation of sentences at the end of the third year. 'That moves that way today because it is broken'; 'You won't get a sandwich because you are naughty'; 'Must take the beds away so I can get out'; 'Dolly disturbed me so I couldn't sleep.' Innumerable relations of space, time, causes and essentialities are grasped here. What, at the beginning of the third year, still lay in dusky twilight and began to brighten only through single points of light, is plunged into clear light. It has become apparent that the things of the world are connected with each other through manifold relations. The categories of Aristotle are revealed to the child as a basis for his thought achievements.

In the child's third year it is really as if the sun of thinking were to appear above the horizon and brightly illuminate the relations that have been formed between all his experiences. The child enters the awakening day of his developing life. Not only objects, but also activities and attributes are included in these relations. Thus Annie, who is a city child and sees canned peas in a shop, comprehends the connection, 'Peas grow in cans, and beans grow in glass,' because she has seen the latter at home preserved in glass jars. Where else should they grow? Four weeks later (at two years and seven months) she is shown a picture of flowers in a meadow and says, 'Little flowers in the meadow ... grow there!'

E. Köhler, full of the impressions gained from observing Annie, writes,

> With the collection of concepts, indeed, in the very midst of the labor of collecting, productive thinking grows from now on through its own law that must determine from within the spiritual development. Threads weave to and fro, everything is related, levelled, separated, discarded, wherever necessary. Judgments lie quite open within reach, even where formulations in speech cannot yet follow.[22]

Thinking even overtakes speech. It runs ahead of it and speech formulations themselves already come partly under the power of the child's own thoughts. It is no longer speech alone that utters the words, but the child's thought experience begins to make use of speech. Movement and speech, which so far have followed rather autocratically their own laws, come under the rulership of contemplation and judgment. Step by step thought becomes king of the soul, whose functions bow down under its light-filled majesty.

That is also the radical difference that exists between walking and speaking, on the one hand, and thinking on the other. Walking and speaking are learned; they unfold step by step and give the child sureness of movement in space and of behaviour in the world of things and beings. Walking enables him to dominate space and speaking to possess the named world around him. Thinking on the other hand, as power of the soul, does not use a manifest bodily tool. It uses neither the limbs, nor the speech organs; it appears like a light, which must have been in existence though it was not visible before. If we should assume it to be created anew in each child, we would be like those who imagine the sun to be a star newly created every morning.

Thinking fills the being of the child from the beginning. It is in existence and at work, but has no possibility as yet to show itself. It dwells in the distant depths of the child's existence, which in the first two years is occupied with the proximity of the body, its sense perceptions, its sensations and feelings. A thorny hedge, behind which thinking is still asleep in the castle of the head, grows out of the manifoldness of these first experiences. It can only occasionally, but sometimes even in earliest babyhood, wake up and appear almost tangibly, though making no utterance. That happens when the dream sleep existence of early childhood is interrupted by a painful illness. Then the eyes of the baby wake up and become the deeply serious messengers of his individuality. I, myself, have often been able to observe this. A mother whose child was operated on at the age of six months, described it once to me as follows. 'She is quiet and peaceful, still serious, but really removed beyond her age — yet entirely human. The baby has almost receded into the background. One must observe this only with respect and love.' Once illness has passed, the infant re-emerges and thinking withdraws until it appears in the course of the third year and begins to perform its activities with the help of speech, memory and fantasy.

Like the sleeping beauty it is then kissed awake by its prince. This is a phenomenon that occurs in every child during the third year and that belongs to the most mysterious events in the realm of the human soul. The individuality of the growing child breaks through the thorny hedge of his daily experiences and awakens his slumbering thinking. In that moment when they behold one another face to face, the consciousness of the individual ego first awakens. This special instant, of which some grown-ups still have a memory, is a turning point in human life. From this moment on an unbroken memory thread exists that carries the continuity of the ego-consciousness. Even if much of it is forgotten in later years, a dim feeling of the unity of one's own person extending back to this point in time remains. Behind it early childhood lies veiled in darkness.

In his autobiography the publisher and writer, Karl Rauch, describes this special moment in a captivating way:

I have a distinct early memory picture of a spring day. I
may have been three years old, a child among children.
The sun was shining, it was late forenoon. Some cousins
were with us on a visit. It must have been one of the
many children's birthdays in the family. We were
romping about among the flower beds and then ran over
a wide piece of ground that was waiting to be dug, right
across the garden to a ditch in which the first green
grasses and herbs were sprouting, while in between the
brownish pink pestilencewort grew exuberantly. I still
know distinctly how I was running, clearly see my older
sister running in front of me as the leader of the whole
host of children who raced ahead, and I feel quite
consciously when I look back today, of how I suddenly
stopped running, looking behind me and recognized
again at some distance behind me the dozen or so other
children, all racing and running. Just as I turned forward
again in the direction of my sister and the ditch, it came
over me, that first consciousness, breaking through as
clear as spirit, of my own self with this thought flashing
up, 'I am I, I — there in front my sister, there behind the
others, but here I, myself, I.' And then the race went on. I
reached my sister, grabbed her quickly by the arm while
running and overtook her. Immediately afterwards all was
again submerged, engulfed by the turmoil of the throng
of children at play ...[23]

Immediately, suddenly and unforeseen this flash of recognition
hit the child's soul in the midst of a wild game and from then on
the consciousness of his own personality remained.

Moriz Carriére described the same phenomenon in the following way.

That I differentiated myself from the world, confronted
the external things and grasped myself as self, occurred
later (after the second year); I stood in the yard on the
street; I could still today show the spot. I was a little
surprised at this event, or rather at this deed.[24]

Jean Paul has described this moment perhaps most beautifully.

> Never will I forget the phenomenon, never told to
> anybody, when I stood at the birth of the consciousness of
> my self, of which I can tell place and time. One morning I
> stood as a very young child at the front door and looked
> left toward a pile of firewood when suddenly the inner
> vision, 'I am an I,' struck down in front of me like a flash
> of lightning from heaven and radiantly remained ever
> since. There my I had seen itself for the first time and
> forever. Deceptions of memory can here hardly be
> thought of, as no tale of strangers could be mixed up with
> what happened nowhere else but behind the veils of the
> holiest of holies of the human soul, the newness of which
> has given permanence to such everyday circumstances.[25]

The poet fully comprehends and recognizes this event that
occurs 'in the holiest of holies of the human soul,' where the
bride of cognition is awakened by the king's son of the individuality. From this moment onward both are united like brother
and sister and so remain until death.

At the awakening of thinking something becomes apparent
that is not so obvious in the case of walking and speaking,
namely, that all three faculties have metamorphosed out of pre-earthly activities in order to appear in the child in an earthly garment. Rudolf Steiner gave concrete indications of this. During
embryonic life these three high human faculties are forming a
chrysalis in order to emerge step by step after birth. Prior to
conception, during pre-natal life, walking, speaking and thinking were three spiritual faculties given to man in his spiritual
existence.

The sleeping thinking awakens at the call of the personality
that finds itself. Whoever remembers this moment sees in full
detail the circumstances then prevailing. Everything down to
the last detail is remembered because the impression is so strong
and lasting that no part of it can be forgotten.

From now on, even the child will speak of himself with full
consciousness as 'I' because he feels that this word is no longer a

name but 'the name of names.' Everything that has a name has also somewhere an 'I.' Man, however, can know this and express this knowledge; he names himself no longer as a thing or a being, but as that innermost part of all being and existence, which in his awakening thinking he has learned to comprehend as 'I.'

The first defiance and birth of the lower ego

Toward the end of the third year when walking, speaking and thinking have been acquired in their fundamental structures, the first phase of childhood development closes and something entirely new takes its place. The child grows into the first age of defiance. Busemann characterizes it as a phase of excitation because feeling and will, working together as affect, step into the foreground and determine the behaviour of the child.[26]

The ego feeling also increases and with it defence and rejection, in the form of defiance, repeatedly break though. Suddenly the child no longer wants to be led. He withdraws his hand from that of the grown-up and stomps off alone. He wants to dress and undress by himself and often refuses to join in play with other children, becoming for a time a 'lone wolf.' Conflicts with the surrounding world pile up and parents and educators without insight and understanding exercise authority and punishment where help and example, gentle guidance and intuitive forgiveness would be the only right attitude. E. Köhler, from her experience with Annie, aptly describes this:

> The child is something new to herself. What is feeling and willing in her is something new to her, from which thinking has not yet gained any distance. Thus, a tremendous contest goes on within her. Once the breakthrough of feeling and willing is over and the almost undifferentiated affect-volition of early childhood has been replaced by the more highly developed feeling and willing, then thinking can free itself from its bondage. If at an earlier stage the child has paved the way toward objectivizing the world, he now continues this objectivization by confronting the world with the 'I' as

something fully recognized, endowed with its own
feeling and willing. It can be called, 'person.' The author
does not think she is wrong in regarding this time of
crisis as the hour when the higher 'I' is born.[27]

However justified this whole description may be, the conclusion arrived at certainly seems unjustified. This time of crisis
mentioned here is not the occasion of the 'I' or ego's birth, but
the result of it. The ego is born in the awakening thinking, and
the result of this even is the age of defiance that now follows.
Neither is it the hour of the birth of the higher ego, but rather
the death of it. What now comes to light is the lower ego, which
will accompany man through the whole of his earthly life.

   Rudolf Steiner has characterized this moment in the light of
spiritual science. He says:

   Clairvoyants, who can trace the spiritual processes
   involved because they have undergone spiritual training,
   discover that something tremendously significant
   happens at the moment when we achieve I-
   consciousness, that is, at the moment of our earliest
   memory. They can see that, during the early years of
   childhood, an aura hovers about us like a wonderful
   human-superhuman power. This aura, which is actually
   our higher part, extends everywhere into the spiritual
   world. But at the earliest moment we can remember, this
   aura penetrates more deeply into our inner being. We can
   experience ourselves as a coherent I from this point on
   because what had previously been connected to the
   higher worlds then entered the I. Thereafter, our
   consciousness establishes its own relationship to the
   outer world.[28]

This is an exact description of the spiritual process that lies hidden behind the events of the period of defiance. The first great
phase of childhood comes to an end, and will and impulse
awaken at the birth of the lower ego.

   We must gradually learn to see this phase of the first three years of childhood in a new light, not like Bühler and his successors who consider the child more or less as an animal that gradually grows out of the 'chimpanzee age' and has overtaken the 'whole phylogenetic animal evolution' by his third year.

Remplein, describing this phase, says,

> In the first phase those impulses and instincts of the body predominate that serve the mere preservation of life, but then they are joined by the impulses furthering the unfolding of the body-soul organism.... This determination by instinct is the predominant characteristic of this whole stage.[29]

If that were the case, the child would learn neither to walk nor to speak and think because these achievements in no way arise from the instinctual nature of the infant. There is no other period in man's life on earth as free from affect or instinct as that of the first three years. The child is an objective rather than a subjective being. Though he rests entirely in himself, develops connections with the surrounding world only slowly, and gradually becomes a personality, he is hardly conscious of himself and therefore not selfish. He is a small world existing in himself, which may expect from the world around everything which seems pleasant and acceptable to him. Where, however, do we find demands or even self-determination in the small child? He accepts what is given and by necessity relinquishes what is withdrawn from him. Rudolf Steiner says:

> In childhood, a dream world still seems to hover about us. We work on ourselves with a wisdom that is *not* in us, a wisdom that is more powerful and comprehensive than all the conscious wisdom we acquire later. This higher wisdom ... is obscured and exchanged for consciousness ...
>
> Something from this world [of the spirit] still flows into our aura during childhood. As individuals we are then directly subject to the guidance of the *entire* spiritual world to which we belong. When we are children up to the moment of our earliest memory — the spiritual

forces from this world flow into us, enabling us to
develop our particular relationship to gravity. At the same
time, the same forces also form our larynx and shape our
brain into living organs for the expression of thought,
feeling, and will.[30]

We meet here with those powers of wisdom that give the child
the faculties of walking, speaking and thinking. In walking he
comes to terms not only with the forces of gravity, by overcoming them, but through this act he separates himself as individual
being from the world of which he was formerly still a part. In
speaking, the child not only learns soul communication with
other human beings but takes possession of things and beings in
a new way so that they belong to him once more. Finally, in
thinking he once more acquires on a higher level what he had
achieved in learning to walk. He lifts himself anew out of the
world, but he is now more firm and consolidated. Like a shepherd he mingles again with the herd, which consists of the
names of all things spread out around him. He has regained
them by giving them names, but now he, himself, must not
remain only a name. He enters the innermost being of the name
by knowing how to name himself beyond his name. This is
called, 'I,' and man thereby recognizes himself as part of the
World-Ego, which as logos, was the origin of all creation.

It was for this reason that Rudolf Steiner said of this time of
the first three years,

> Most meaningfully, therefore, the I-being of Christ is
> expressed in the words: '*I am the Way, the Truth, and the
> Life!*' The higher spiritual forces form our organism in
> childhood — though we are not conscious of this — so
> that our body becomes the expression of the way, the
> turth and the life. Similarly, the human spirit gradually
> becomes the *conscious* bearer of the way, the truth and the
> life by permeating itself with Christ.[31]

Chapter 4

The Unfolding of the Three Highest Senses

The senses of speech and thought

When we approach the question of how the human spirit unfolds in the course of early childhood with real courage, a special problem strikes us at once. We meet one of those great questions that appear repeatedly as hurdles for the thinker's courage to take in a high jump.

This problem is the every new miracle that comes to pass at the beginning of the child's second year: The spoken word is not only heard, but also grasped as a sign and its meaning understood. This understanding occurs long before the child has developed the power of thinking! Thus, an intellectual activity is performed before the development of the faculties necessary for it. This is a miracle that impresses everyone except the psychologist who is lacking in philosophical training. Yet, one of the most difficult questions of child psychology is how it is truly possible that words can be grasped and their meaning understood even in earliest childhood. In his fundamental investigations of the development of speech in the child, W. Stern has drawn our attention to a most important rule, which he formulated in the following way:

From the innumerable words that the child continually hears, his mind makes an unconscious selection by discarding most and retaining only a few. This selection is twofold. The majority of rejected words are 'beyond understanding,' and of these a smaller number have been

rejected as 'beyond speech.' The retardation of what can
be said with what can be understood is a peculiarity that
continues even in adult years ... but nowhere is the
difference as striking as in the first months of speech.'[1]

Stern points to that threshold erected between hearing and
understanding the spoken word. In the course of the first year
the child hears a great number of words and sentences, but does
not yet comprehend them as independent parts, because they
are still embedded in the 'experience landscapes' of which I have
spoken in the second chapter of this book. Only at the end of
the first and at the beginning of the second year does the word
appear as symbol and as bearer of meaning in the child's realm
of consciousness.

These first words, or better, syllabic complexes, are not yet
true words with sense and meaning, but are only the expression
of something that the child wants to indicate. The syllabic
sequences are mostly still onomatopoeic designations like
'splash-splash' for bathing, 'bow-wow' for dog, 'yum-yum' for
eating, etc. The child associates experienced values of feeling
with them. When he says, 'Tick-tock,' he may point to the clock,
though without having grasped that he is saying the name of the
object. As long as the period of one-word sentences and syllabic
complexes lasts, that is, until about the middle of the second
year, something spoken is only expression or interpretation,
such as pointing to an object or an event.

Nevertheless, we should play close attention to what
appears here because it is a kind of preparatory step toward
true word understanding. The spoken word is distinguished
from all other forms of sound production and is felt and
noticed as speech. Tone and sound have become differentiated.
This is the first threshold, which leads to a further understanding of the spoken word. The crossing of the second
threshold will begin when the child proceeds from the period
of saying to that of naming.

When, at about eighteen months, the joy of asking for the
names of things, and then of pronouncing and using these
names himself awakens for the child, the understanding of

words begins and speech first assumes its rights. These fundamental differentiations have already been pointed out by Husserl and later by Scheler. Scheler's efforts have been especially helpful toward achieving clarity in this field:

> Between expression and speech the phenomenological findings show an absolute abyss.... Already the existence of a tone, sound or noise complex as 'sound' — and though it be only 'one sound' outside in the passage, 'one sound' in the woods — requires that I perceive in this complex something more than its sense content that is 'expressed' in it, that is 'proclaimed aloud' in it. A 'sound,' therefore, is already something quite different from tone, noise or a so-called association of such a complex with an imagined object. But the 'sound' still tarries in the sphere of pure expression ... a whole world separates even the most primitive word from mere expression. The entirely new thing that appears in the word is the fact that it does not, like the expression, merely point back to an experience, but in its primary function it points outward to an object in the world. The word 'means' something that has nothing to do either with its sound-body, or with the experience of feelings, thoughts and ideas that it may express besides ... The word appears to us as the fulfillment of a demand made by the object itself. It appears in the understanding as a simple rather than a complex whole, which only the reflective analysis of the philologist or psychologist may later differentiate into the sound and the sense aspect (the 'word body' and 'word sense').[2]

I quote Scheler's statements at length because they go to the roots of a differentiation and separation to which Rudolf Steiner drew attention repeatedly and which in the future will become of fundamental importance for an understanding of the human being. It is significant that Scheler chooses his essay, *On the Idea of Man*, in which to come to grips with the problem of understanding and speaking.

Later, Binswanger tried to approach these problems from the

standpoint of the neurologist and psychiatrist. He opens his essay, *On the Problem of Speaking and Thinking*, with the following statement:

> A homogenous phenomenon is the basis of the problem of speech and thought, from the simple, meaningful spoken or written word to speech proper, which in agreement with Husserl, we wish to call the sense-enlivened or sense-full expression. If we analyze this phenomenon, an undertaking that belongs to phenomenology, we can differentiate first the articulated complex of sounded or written, physical signs; second, the psychic experiences in which man lends sense or meaning to these signs — the sense-giving and intentional actions; third, the ideal, logical sense or the meaning itself through which the expression points to an object or 'means' it.[3]

Though much in this formulation is incorrect and generalized, the reference to the three realms, physical, psychic and logical, clearly expresses the fact that speech must be understood only as a unity, as the synthesis of bodily, soul and spiritual relations. But as a result of this, to grasp and comprehend what is spoken must also be threefold. Whether I read what is written, or hear what is spoken, or whether I grasp signs and gestures, it is never an action of body and soul alone. If it were only that, no under-standing through speech could ever come about.

The miracle already mentioned in which the first under-standing of the heard word begins to dawn in the small child, presupposes that the spiritual part of the childlike human being is precisely what is involved in the process of comprehending, and that even in earliest infancy a threshold of understanding is crossed that creates a real word from a sound formation.

Otherwise, how should it be possible that the small child, seemingly without the slightest difficulty, begins to understand the word as sound gesture and directly grasps its hidden sense? A spiritual deed is the basis of such an event. Scheler and Husserl tried to point to this but in spite of the keenest observation of the phenomena in question they were not able to solve this riddle.

Rudolf Steiner, however, reached a comprehensive answer to this problem by laying the foundation of a new theory of the senses. As early as 1909 he described how the understanding of the spoken word should not be counted among the acts of cognition but among the sense activities. He showed how even to hear a spoken word is more than merely hearing and that a special sense underlies this faculty. He called this a speech or word sense and the understanding of the spoken word, the concept or thought sense. In the first descriptions of his theory of the senses he says:

> So we come to a ninth sense. We discover it when we ponder on the fact that in man there resides in truth a faculty of perception that does not rest on judgment but is nevertheless present within it. It is what we perceive when we enter into communication with our fellow men through speech. A true sense, the speech sense, underlies what is conveyed to us through speech ... The child learns speech before it learns to judge.[4]

And further on:

> By means of the concept sense, man is able while perceiving the concept, which does not clothe itself in the spoken sound, to understand it. In order that we may be able to form a judgment we must have concepts. If the soul is to be active, it must first be able to perceive the concept. To do so, it requires the concept sense, which is just as much a sense in itself as either the sense of smell or the sense of taste.

Here a fundamentally new thought directs our previously existing views on the development of the human spirit along entirely unaccustomed paths. Not only a great number of existing problems can be solved with this,* but at the same time, new questions

---

* For example, all the problems of the riddle of aphasia can be gradually brought nearer to a solution through these ideas, and from this starting point the burning questions of the disturbances of reading and writing in childhood can be met with real understanding.

emerge that hitherto have hardly come into the light of our attention and awareness. In his book, *Riddles of the Soul*, Steiner discussed in detail Franz Brentano's psychology and then added a
special chapter, *The True Basis of Intentional Relation*. In it he develops important aspects of his theory of the senses. The following
paragraph is particularly significant to our present considerations:

> One believes, for example, that it would be sufficient,
> when hearing the words of another person to speak only
> of sense to the extent that it comes into question through
> hearing alone, leaving everything else to be ascribed to a
> non-sensuous inner activity. But this is not so. In the
> hearing of words and their understanding as thoughts, a
> threefold activity is involved. Every member of this
> threefold activity must be considered by itself for a truly
> scientific comprehension to be established. 'Hearing' is
> an activity, but 'hearing' by itself is as little a 'taking in of
> words' (*Vernehmen*) as 'touching' is a 'seeing.' Just as it is
> relevant to distinguish between the sense of "touch" and
> that of 'sight,' so also is it relevant to distinguish between
> that of 'hearing,' and that of 'taking in words,' and the
> further sense of 'grasping thoughts.' It leads to a faulty
> psychology and theory of knowledge, if one does not
> sharply distinguish between the 'grasping of thoughts'
> and the activity of thinking without recognizing the sense
> character of the former. One makes this mistake only
> because the organs for 'taking in words' and for 'grasping
> thoughts' are not externally as perceptible as the ear for
> 'hearing.' In reality, organs exist for these two perceptual
> activities just as the ear exists for 'hearing.'[5]

In this description Steiner brings into correct focus what we
have described above in regard to Binswanger's exposition.
What is shown there as physical sign, as psychic experience and
as logical sense, is basically a sense experience occurring in three
differentiated sense realms. The physical sign is transmitted by
the ear as the word that is heard, or by the eye as the word that is
read. The psychic experience is the 'taking in of the word,' and

the logical sense, the 'grasping of the thought.' How challenging are Rudolf Steiner's formulations to psychology and philosophy! They represent an entirely new phase in the history of the psychology and philosophy of speech and many critical investigations will have to be made to do justice to this tremendous impulse. Above all, the physiology of the senses will have to find a new orientation and entirely transform the views on the spiritual development of the child. The remaining sections of this chapter are meant to be a first attempt in this direction.

The development of the word sense and thought sense

There can hardly be any doubt that the word sense (comprehension of the spoken word) and the thought sense (comprehension of concepts) both develop in the child during the first two years, if his development takes a fairly normal course. At the end of the first year the child already begins to use one-word sentences with understanding and to comprehend some of the words addressed to him. At the end of the second year, when he begins to say two- or three-word sentences, he already knows a large number of words, recognizes their sense and meaning and can use them accordingly. The word as formation and sign has become his permanent possession. He has made the first roots of language his own, but has been able to achieve this only because the senses of speech and thought have awakened in him.

To gain some understanding of these two senses it will be necessary to study their development in connection with that of the child's speech. The unfolding of language in the child must be intimately connected with the acquisition of these two senses because it is obvious that the newborn child possesses neither word nor thought sense. Both certainly are present as predispositions, but the development of speech is needed to turn them into faculties.

In the second chapter of this book we pointed out that the first year is of the greatest importance for the formation of speech. We said that the development of speech begins with the first cry and after that the baby soon starts to utter a great variety of sounds. He cries and crows, gurgles and coos, and at the end of the first month most mothers have learned to 'understand' the various sounds and noises. For example, Valentine, an accurate observer, writes,

> At the end of the first month I could distinguish three types of sounds. First, the cry of hunger, which was restless and sharp, increased each time and after the last strong outbreak suddenly ceased. Second, the cry of pain, which was a much stronger and more lasting cry. Third, a satisfied contented gurgling, which was different in its sound formation in the three children observed.[6]

The cry in this instance is nothing but statement. It is an expression of well-being or misery and as yet has hardly any reference to the speaking environment as such. This relationship, however, is already being established in the second or third month. About this Valentine writes, 'When father or mother chatted to the baby, humming was returned in reply. That happened with Y. on the twenty-second, with B. on the thirty-second and with A. on the forty-ninth day for the first time. Thus speech development was even at this time connected with social relationships.' Valentine mentions that some observers put the beginning of this 'responding' on the part of the baby later, especially when the children did not come under observation in their family milieu. But most found that it began around the middle or end of the second month.

Here we witness how the baby reacts with understanding upon being addressed for the first time. He answers the speech of another person with his own utterance. He responds and indicates that in his imitation he uses the same organ as his example. In this we can see a first understanding for the act of speaking.

In the course of the third month the sounds and tones that the child utters become quite diversified and consist of recognizable consonants as well as vowels. Again Valentine says, 'By this stage of three months it became quite evident from the number of sounds made by these children, which we could never have pronounced, that the speech of the child was largely independent of the words he heard.' This is a further and most important conclusion because it shows that the hearing at this infantile age does not yet work together with the activities of the larynx and other speech organs. The child hears with his ears, and independently of this he makes utterances with his larynx and the other developing speech organs. The 'intentional relations' between these two activities have not yet developed and only another person can make the baby's speech organs respond when he addresses him directly.

From about the fourth month on, however, the infant begins to imitate sounds and noises he has heard and, once he has achieved them, to make them his own by continued exercise. Now the time begins when during waking hours children babble continually and keep repeating certain sounds and sound complexes. Around the sixth month, this 'conscious' imitation of sounds he has heard becomes a daily event. The infant has now reached the stage when ear and speech organs can work as a functional whole. This is an important step, and a prattling comprehension of the sounds of his native language begins.

Valentine describes a most striking phenomenon that he observed in his own children and that thousands of other fathers and mothers may also have observed without noticing. He points out that the sounds imitated at will are always spoken only in a whisper. He says, 'These deliberate imitations, however, were strikingly different from the spontaneous and the deferred imitative speaking. They were whispered.'[7] This behaviour occurs at about the eighth month.

Preyer also describes whispering by his child in whom it occurred in the tenth or eleventh months. He says, 'When I spoke, the child, observing my lips attentively, often made the attempt to speak after me. Usually some different sound came forth, however, or there was merely a soundless movement of the lips.'[8] This description makes it clear why only whispering or silent lip movements occur. The child looks at the movements of the grown-up's mouth and imitates the movement but not the sounds. He can indeed prattle aloud unconsciously and unconsciously imitate the sounded tones of speech. Conscious repetition, however, occurs at first only in the interaction of his observation of mouth movements, that is, the interaction between his eyes and his motor impulses.

Toward the end of the first year a significant new step is taken in development. Preyer, in describing it, points out that the child not only reacts to tones, noises and sounds at this time, but may also turn in the direction of the speaker when his name is called. At every new sound that he has not yet heard he is astonished and shows this by opening his eyes and mouth wide. By frequently repeating the words, 'Shake hands,' and simultaneously holding out his hand, Preyer even induced his child to comply with this request. The beginning of word memory was thereby established.

Most other observers are in agreement with these conclusions that toward the end of the first year a few words are understood and the movements corresponding to them are executed. Thus, Valentine's child Y. was able to look at the floor when hearing the word, 'kitty,' in order to search for it, and at the word, 'birdie,' to look at the wall where birds were depicted on the wallpaper. He also understood the words, 'bottle,' 'mouth,' 'bye-bye,' and a few others and performed characteristic gestures relative to them.

W. Stern relates the following of his child, Eva, when twelve and thirteen months old.

> We are continually astounded and can scarcely keep up
> with her development. It is hardly credible at her age.
> One day she will grasp the meaning of a word a little, the
> next, a little more, the following day she will understand
> it entirely. All at once we noticed that the child
> understood perfectly what we said.[9]

Similarly, Preyer remarks,

> The most important progress consists in the awakened
> understanding of spoken words. The ability to learn has
> emerged almost overnight. Suddenly, it did not require
> constant repetition of the question, 'How tall is the
> child?' at the same time lifting her arms in order to get
> her to make the movement each time she heard, 'How
> tall,' or 'all,' or even, 'a.'[10]

When we try to interpret these details of the child's speech development during the first year with regard to the word sense as well as the thought sense, we can note a steady development. At first, the sound utterances of the child are entirely spontaneous and only an expression of the experience of his own existence. In the second month, the child responds by humming when spoken to. He becomes dimly aware of the movements of his own mouth. This is a sense perception that belongs in the realm of motor sensations and is concentrated in the region of the mouth.

In the third month the variety of sounds and tones that the child can produce spontaneously is extended, and from the fourth month on he begins to imitate definite sounds that he has heard. This ability is more firmly established in the course of the following months, with no new fundamental acquisition being added until the seventh or eighth months. About this time the child begins to imitate at will the words and sounds spoken to him. This imitation primarily involves the interaction of eyes and lips, and is related to the lip reading of the deaf and dumb, which has its origin here. This process, therefore, takes place softly or quite voicelessly. A combination of the sense of sight with motor sensation, which produces movement of the mouth, is also present, bringing about a further development of consciousness in the region of the lips and mouth. Thus, another step is taken in the development of the ability to respond.

Toward the end of the first year, beginning at about the ninth month, a kind of intuitive comprehension of the word as designation arises. Many authors speak of this as a 'word understanding,' but that is by no means the case. As shown above, all these 'understood' words are clothed in gestures that imitate repeated sound structures. These sound structures are certainly remembered but not yet understood. Memory alone enables the child to experience a sound structure as a speech symbol and to connect it with the respective gestures, sensations and objects. When little Eva Stern at thirteen months used the word, 'doll,' for her doll and all pictures of children, it was a recognition of definitely established connections. These were by no means identifications for her that revealed a 'name' through word or sound structure. It was rather a case in which the child was able to remember and recognize definite, self-chosen sound formations and words. One should not fall into the error of considering this accomplishment to be a form of the cognitive process. It is a simple recognition and not an understanding of the word and its meaning. Nevertheless, it is a new achievement of great importance to the further development of speech.

Anyone familiar with the teaching and education of deaf children knows that one of the greatest and often insurmountable difficulties is to awaken in the deaf and dumb their sleeping word memory. They learn relatively soon to hear and differentiate tones and sounds but the difficulties experienced in 'marking,' 'be-thinking,' and 'recollecting' words represent one of the greatest obstacles to the acquisition of somewhat normal colloquial speech. The hearing child achieves these abilities 'suddenly' and 'overnight.' But this happens only at that time when the child has acquired his upright position. Word and sound memory awaken only after the development of uprightness.

While the word is consciously separated for the first time, it is sorted out in a twofold way. On the one hand, the word is lifted out of the realm of other sounds and noises and remembered independently. On the other hand, however, it is drawn away from the motor sphere and treated as an independent world. All these observations demonstrate that in the course of the first year the child gradually learns to experience word and sound formations, and then comes to know them at the beginning of the second year as self-contained entities. At the time when he raises himself from gravity, the word also emerges from the motor organism and from the other sounds with which it was formerly intermingled. The liberations of two activities have occurred simultaneously. The child has learned to stand upright on the earth, and, when the child begins to speak, the word rises up like a lark into the free and breathing air.

When, together with the acquisition of the upright position, the word also gains its independence, the word sense is born. With its separation from the other motor and sensory regions, the word, although not yet recognized in its independent form as thought, is received like a sense perception. The faculty of word memory is indeed already the result of the developed word sense. Here, at the beginning of the second year, stands the cradle of the word sense. Rudolf Steiner expresses it in the following words. 'Because sound sensation precedes the forming of judgment, the child learns to feel the meaning of the sounds of words before he reaches the use of judgment. At the hand of speech the child learns to judge.'[11]

Now, from direct experience communicated to him by the speech sense, the child knows that a word is different from any other sound that reaches him through hearing. The word is born as an independent entity and is laid into the cradle of the word sense.

The child occupies the next six months practicing the use of the newly acquired sense of word or speech. He does not learn many additional new words and sound structures, but rather makes his own what has suddenly been achieved. Therefore, remarkably few new words are acquired during this period.

At this time, too, the acquisition and development of a special faculty occurs. This is important because it points to the awakened sense of speech. Valentine writes,

> I have already mentioned that in B. and Y. only two examples of true gesture language appeared before the end of the first year. It is well-known that the deaf and dumb develop an extensive language of gestures to compensate for the absence of a language of sound. An experienced teacher of deaf and dumb children told me that lip reading and attempts to speak are delayed in deaf children if gestures are allowed to continue. There are also records of children who continued gesture language because of slowness in acquiring speech ... Among the Dionne quintuplets gestures were remarkably expressive and fairly common, and these children were actually retarded in speech.[12]

Valentine then gives many examples of how, after the completion of the first year, sound and gesture language can vicariously replace each other.

The following words of Rudolf Steiner should be considered in this context:

> We must also take into account that audible tone is not alone in revealing to us an inwardness such as that present in tone of speech. In the end, gestures, mimicry, and facial expressions also lead us to something simple and direct that must be included, along with the content of any audible tone, in the domain of the sense of word.[13]

This is a confirmation of the fact that true gestures begin to appear as gesture language only after the birth of the sense of speech.*

All onomatopoeic sounds that the child begins to use are not really words but sound gestures, repeated in imitation of sound he has heard, especially in imitation of words spoken to him. The memory of sound becomes more fixed and is combined with perceptions from other sensory realms, especially that of the eye. Picture books can now be read because the child takes the greatest delight in connecting their illustrations with the words belonging to them. The word, it is true, is not yet 'understood,' but it is remembered; it has become perception and idea. Because the word sense has developed as sense activity, it has begun to perceive the word and to transform this perception into an idea.

When in the second half of the second year the child enters the first age of questioning and makes such startling progress in the second stage of speech development, when he begins to ask the names of things and beings and acquires the new words as quickly as possible by simple repetition, it seems as if true thought action might be appearing in the child. Thus, W. Stern writes:

> The occurrence just described must undoubtedly be considered as a mental act of the child in the real sense of

---

* What exists today as 'Gestalt' Psychology, frequently quite misunderstood, has its roots here in the sense of speech. This, however, can be discussed only in a much wider setting.

the word. The insight into the relation between sign and import that the child gains here is something fundamentally different from simply dealing with perceptions and their associations. The demand that some name must belong to every object, whatever its nature, may be considered as a real — perhaps the child's first — general thought.[14]

Stern, however, though he comes from the school of Brentano and Husserl, falls victim to one of those fatal confusions that lead to incomprehension of the independently active thought sense. It is impossible to expect from a two-year-old child a 'general' act of thinking, and to imagine that he logically comprehends that every thing has a name. Though the child later becomes aware of this fact, it is due not to an act of cognition but to one of perception when the word sense is joined by the thought sense. Rudolf Steiner says, 'Indeed, there also exists a *direct and immediate perception* for that which is revealed in a concept, so that we must speak of a *sense of concept*. What we can experience within our own soul as a concept, we can also receive as revealed from an external being.'[15]

It is this that begins to be unveiled in the two-year-old child. The words become gates and windows for looking into the world of ideas, and he can perceive these ideas even if he cannot yet think them.

Stern also points out that with 'naming,' the third root of speech tendency, the 'intentional' one as he calls it, begins to work. But these intentional relations are acts that occur between the different sense regions. They are not soul processes belonging to the region of thought. When seen from another side, it becomes even clearer that we are concerned here with an awakening — one could almost say, the first dawning of the thought sense. In the second part of these investigations we dealt briefly with the so-called 'change of meaning' of words in this phase of development. We drew attention to the fact that these are by no means chance designations but that children draw the contours of a comprehensive concept as an idea much more ingeniously than grown-ups are able to do. Valentine[16] gives some relevant examples of fundamental importance, to each of which I have added the necessary comments:

'E.W. uses at fifteen months (!) the word, "door," for doors, garden gates and water taps.' Here we have a grasp of things that can be 'opened.' This is a much wider concept than the single words would indicate by themselves. The idea of 'opening' is represented by the word, 'door.'

'B. at nineteen months first calls a sparrow, "dickie," and then all birds, later still all flies, spiders and bits of fluff floating in the air.' Again we have a comprehensive idea, 'flying,' and the name 'dickie' is given to everything that flies or has the potentiality of flying.

'B. at twenty months first says, "go(ne)" when objects disappear or food is finished. He says it again when he has had enough food and pushes the rest away.' The passive use of 'go' becomes an active one produced at will. The meaning has not changed at all; it was well-defined from the beginning, but always broad and general.

Another child[17] at seventeen months uses the word 'eije-bapp,' (for *eisenbahn,* railway), which until then was a designation only for his toy railway, and for some dogs lined up in a row. Here we can easily discover the identity of form impressions and their naming with the same word. But we cannot call this deeds of thinking, but identifications that show the 'idea' of a word to have been grasped, but grasped as form, as perception. On the other hand, there are also many instances where the comprehension of the idea of a word has been too narrow, when a child, for instance, applies the word 'armchair' only to one definite type of chair, but does not recognize those of unfamiliar form.

Many more examples could be given but the principle presented here shows that at about eighteen months the child begins to develop his thought sense in addition to the already perfected sense of speech. This sense activity starts rather abruptly and suddenly because the thought sense is awakened at the moment when the names of things have become experience. It might also be said that at the moment the thought sense awakens in the child all things receive a name. In this way, by becoming bearers of names, words assume their meaning. The further development of the thought sense occurs in a slightly different form from that of the sense of speech, which grows firmer and stronger because no new words were acquired. In the case of the thought sense, however, a rapid acquisition of new words occurs making it possible to grasp as comprehensively as possible the images of ideas in all their manifoldness.

These images of ideas can be conceived by the child either more broadly or more narrowly than in their later correspondence to fully developed speech. They are, however, in no way arbitrary. They only differ in dimension, which is directly related to the child's breadth or narrowness, that is, with the breadth of his soul existence, which expands beyond his true being, and with the narrowness of his earthly bodily existence in which he is a little child. This continues its expression right into the awakening and handling of the thought sense.

One of the most moving examples of the awakening of the thought sense can be seen in the way the seven-year-old Helen Keller suddenly grasped an understanding of words. Her teacher, Miss Sullivan, reports:

We went out to the pumphouse, and I made Helen hold her mug under the spout while I pumped. As the cold water gushed forth, filling the mug, I spelled 'w-a-t-e-r' into Helen's free hand. The word coming so close upon the sensation of cold water rushing over her hand seemed to startle her. She dropped the mug and stood as one transfixed. A new light came over her face. She spelled 'w-a-t-e-r' several times. Then she dropped to the ground, asking for the name of the earth and that of the pump and trellis. Suddenly turning around, she asked for my name. I spelled, 'teacher.' At this moment the nurse came to the pumphouse with Helen's little sister. Helen spelled, 'baby,' and pointed to the nurse. This was the first time she used a word spelled out as means of communication by herself. On the way back to the house she was in great excitement and learned the name of every object she touched so that she had added some thirty new words to her vocabulary within a few hours. Some of them were, 'door,' 'open,' 'shut,' 'give,' 'go,' and 'come.'[18]

The next morning Miss Sullivan added a postscript to the letter she had written the previous evening. It read,

> Helen got up this morning like a radiant fairy. She flew from one object to another, asked for the names of everything and, full of joy, kissed me. Last night when she went to bed, quite on her own she snuggled into my arms and kissed me for the first time. I thought my heart would break, so full of joy was it.

Here we must bear in mind that for weeks previous the teacher of this deaf-blind child had inscribed the names of things into her hand in sign language. The child could repeat them, but she could not grasp or perceive them. They were signs without meaning. Her speech sense existed as gesture sense. Suddenly, however, as if by revelation, her thought sense awakened and from that moment — that world moment — on her spirit being was at home on earth.[19] She could, like Adam, call things by their names. A new light transfigured her face because the light of the spirit had awakened in her and radiated from her.

A similar joy, which is not so immediate because it does not awake so suddenly, also illuminates the two-year-old child. He is accepted here on earth as a human being through the fact that he can comprehend the names of things. He has become an Adam.

The physical organ of the sense of speech

Now that we have described the unfolding of the senses of speech and of thought in the light of speech development, we can take a further step toward an understanding of these phenomena.

It is indeed new and somewhat startling to have to accept the fact that everything hitherto regarded as a complicated act of thinking is reduced to a simple sense experience. Thus, a small child does not think the meaning of the words he acquires but perceives it through his senses. This may be difficult to accept because the words, 'sentient' or 'sense experience,' are so narrowly bound up with our habitual way of thinking about them. For us, 'sense,' or 'sentient,' is everything connected with those experiences that we have in the outer world, where we see and hear, smell and taste the qualities of the things we perceive.

We also have sensations of pain, hunger and thirst, and we dimly experience our equilibrium in space and the position of our limbs relative to each other. These are sense experiences that we continually receive. With them our sensation of life and existence is most intimately connected. These sense perceptions, however, are experiences that, although vague and dull and not entering directly the field of consciousness, are nevertheless significant. For the loss of equilibrium or a disturbance in feeling the position of our limbs, or also diminished sensation of pain can lead to the most serious impairment of our existence. They are at least symptoms of deep-seated illness. These sense experiences of our body and soul conditions, to which we must add our feelings of well-being or discomfort, belong to the sphere of sense processes.

Even for the latter we can still accept the word 'sentient' in its general characterization. Our body is only part of the 'outer world' and we can experience it as such by means of a special group of senses. We not only see it partly from outside and hear it speak and sing, but we feel its condition quite directly in pleasure and pain, in being well or unwell, and we know this to be so not only for ourselves but for everyone.

How is something supposed to become the content of our senses that lies beyond the 'sense' world and reveals itself only as thought? It is still possible to retain some of the 'sense' character of the perception in the word sense, since this represents only a kind of widened sense of hearing. What is revealed in hearing as a single sound or tone becomes, in the homogeneous perception of a sound, complex in the word sense.

In the sound of a vowel or consonant many single sounds are joined that the word sense (or sense of speech) comprehends as a whole, as a homogeneous form. Just as through the sense of hearing we can grasp a melody from single tones, so through the medium of the sense of speech we can perceive a word or succession of words from the joining of single sounds.

After this has happened, another sphere is opened and through the word we are supposed to sense and perceive the meaning it expresses. Everything that precedes this process in the field of perception is of a different character, since a thing or a being tastes, smells, has colour and form, utters tones and sounds — all of which are qualities of its existence. Even the name it bears still belongs to it and is part of its character and existence. The idea, the concept that is it, itself, however, is not a part or a portion, but much more than that. It is something indivisible, the 'ens' itself. It can well bear different names, it can be called, 'dog,' but it can also be called, canis, chien, or, Hund. It can have many such names, just as it can have an infinite number of attributes. But 'the' dog, the dog-hood is contained in each name, in each attribute so that it is a uniform whole in all its differentiation. Is this indivisibleness, however, this being, which, when it is we, ourselves, we designate with the word, 'I,' supposed to be given to us as perception, so that not only qualities but even the bearer of these qualities is supposed to become our immediate experience?

Yet how should an understanding be possible between men if this immediate experience did not exist? Can it be imagined that thinking can be measured in any other way except by the perception of concepts and ideas? The prevailing view that from our manifold experiences we gain the necessary concepts through gradual abstraction cannot be upheld. We can only begin to comprehend the miracle of word understanding in the child, if in our consistent investigation of the spheres of the senses we also include those that bring to our experience not only the qualities of the things but their *ens* itself.

When this is understood, a further, weighty problem confronts us that results from the question, If for every sense process hitherto known, an organ can be found in the body, where do the senses of speech and thought have their physical organization? Nothing is known about this even though there is no part of our body that has not been thoroughly investigated anatomically down to the last detail. Since it is a case of sense processes, however, we must ask about the sense organs pertaining to them. Only after these have been found, examined and investigated, can the senses of speech and thought reveal themselves as 'comprehensible' entities.

In his *Riddles of the Soul*, Rudolf Steiner outlined the nature of the senses of speech and thought and added the following remarks:

> It leads to a faulty psychology and theory of knowledge if one does not sharply distinguish between the 'grasping of thoughts' and the activity of thinking, and fails to recognize the sense character of the former. One makes this mistake because the organ for 'taking in' words *(vernehmen)* and that for 'grasping' thoughts are not externally as perceptible as the ear for 'hearing.' In truth, there exist 'organs' for these two perceptive activities just as the ear exists for 'hearing.'[20]

The spiritual investigator, as we see, has no doubts about the existence of physical organs either for word sense or thought sense and these two functions can become really effective only through them. Is it at all possible to find these organs in the multitude of the morphological structures of the human body? So far no one in science has even thought of these two senses, let alone tried to assign working organs to them. It could be, however, that the functions of certain well-known morphological structures have been misinterpreted and activities attributed to them that they do not really perform. In other words, special parts of our body could be the organs of our senses of thought and speech that have not yet been recognized as such because these senses themselves are still unknown.

If this surmise is true, it will not be a question of finding a 'new' organ because the human body has been completely investigated macroscopically as well as microscopically. What will be necessary is a new interpretation of the existing organ and tissue structures so that they appear in a new order and shape. Then a number of organs to which no common basic design has hitherto been attributed may be recognized that will form the physical organization we hope to find. Here we have reached an important point of departure to which we want to hold fast for the time being.

Looking back on our past considerations, we found that the unfolding of the sense of speech occurs exactly at the end of the first year, and the thought sense breaks through in the course of the second year. In these periods of development the child acquires an upright position, the ability to walk and the faculty of speech. Does the sense of speech appear at the end of the first year because it is intimately bound up with the acquisition of the ability to walk? Indeed, is it not conceivable that man's ability to walk upright is the prerequisite for the sense of speech? Could this perhaps be the reason why so many children who have difficulties in acquiring an upright position also find it so hard to acquire speech and speech understanding? Is this the reason why an intimate connection exits between man's motor activities and his sense of speech? Can only the acquisition of the ability to walk upright build the organ that then acts as the sense organ for the understanding of words?

A serious consideration of such questions can lead to the further deliberation that the acquisition of walking, as described in the first chapter of this book, is the product of man's gradually gaining control of his voluntary muscles by means of his self. In the course of the first year, this process builds up a distinct organ as part of our nervous system that is called the 'pyramidal system.' It consists of groups of nerves that extend from the voluntary muscles of the limbs and the trunk into the spinal cord, where they come in contact with another group of nerves running up the spinal cord and terminating in definite locations in the cortical regions of the cerebrum. This whole complex of nerves, extending from the cortex via the spinal cord to the single muscles, is described as the pyramidal system. It is a highly complex and extensive organ, which constitutes an essential part of our nervous system.

Until quite recently, physiologists and neurologists were firmly convinced that this was a group of motor nerves that caused voluntary muscular movements. Of late, however, strong objections have been raised against this conception both in physiology and neurology. Clinical observations of the ill and the results of extensive brain operations have shown that these motor nerves function as such only under certain conditions. Movements that are experimentally induced through these nerves differ decidedly in form and character from normal movements, which are suppressed by artificial stimulation of the pyramidal system.[21] Modern neurology is thus faced with a riddle, which at present it hardly dares to admit, let alone to try to solve. This most 'human' of all nerve groupings, collectively called the 'pyramid path,' is functionally unrecognized today. We know its pathological performance when it fails through injury or illness, but its normal function is veiled in darkness.

Thus we see in the pyramidal system a morphological entity, a group of nerves that apparently does not perform the function hitherto assigned to it. Though closely connected with voluntary movements, it certainly is not the cause of them. This morphological entity is formed during the first year of life, but once its formation is completed it seems to be no longer directly connected with the functional achievement of walking upright and the voluntary mobility associated with it. The nerve apparatus thus formed has taken an intimate part in the acquisition of the ability to walk upright, but when this is achieved, it begins to place itself at the disposal of new functions. This is a form of functional change that should be noted.

Rudolf Steiner gives a description in which he explains the nature and form of the physical organ of the sense of speech:

> Insofar as we have the power to move and to put into action everything we have within ourselves as movement, when we move our hands, or nod our head, for example — insofar as we have these forces to set our body into motion, their lies within us as the basis for this faculty of movement a physical organism. And this is not the physical organism of life, but of the faculty of movement.[22]

Steiner means something quite specific here. He is not referring to movement that appears as voluntary motor activity, but to the physical organization through which mobility manifests itself. Is he not referring to the pyramidal system? This system, as we have seen, is not the cause of voluntary movements, yet they are executed in connection with it. Then Steiner adds:

> This [organism of the faculty of movement] is at the same time the organ of perception for speech, for words that are addressed to us by others. We could not understand words if we did not have in us this physical apparatus for movement. It is really true that to the extent that the nerves go out from our central nervous system to all our organs of movement, we also find there the sense apparatus for words that are spoken to us.[23]

These words only confirm what I have tried to describe above because the nerves that 'go from our central nervous system to all our organs of movement' are without doubt the nerves of the pyramidal system. We have, therefore, to seek the sense organ of the sense of speech in the pyramidal path and in the nerve structures belonging to it. Here is a thousandfold instrument whose strings are strung between the muscles and the brain and in their totality serve our understanding of speech.

This view has been confirmed by clinical research carried out by the director of the Neurological Clinic in Hamburg. K. Conrad made extensive investigations in the localization of certain speech disturbances in the brain.[24] He was able to show that these aphasic disturbances occur at the time when the cerebrum has been injured or destroyed in those parts known to be the regions in which the pyramidal system has its origin, and that these aphasic disturbances are mostly those that have to do with a partial or complete loss of speech understanding. Such patients are either unable to understand words addressed to them or they lose the faculty of speaking. The latter state is conditioned by the fact that the comprehension of word forms has been preserved only in part or not at all.

We have now gained a fundamental insight into the phenomenology of the sense of speech. We have recognized its intimate connection with the acquisition of the ability to walk upright and have described its physical organ, which is a purely nervous one consisting only of nerve tissue. The entire system of voluntary muscles is found at the ends of the nerves, and though it is held together by the pyramidal system, it is neither functionally activated nor moved by it. The pyramidal path has become the organ of the word sense through the fact that it belongs to the voluntary motor apparatus as a whole, yet does not move it. On the contrary, it rests quietly within itself. This is the change of function that has occurred here.

Rudolf Steiner describes this:

> Suppose I make this movement (hand raised in defence) ...
> The capacity to make this movement, to the extent it
> comes out of my entire organism of movement, causes
> something quite specific because not even the smallest
> movement is localized in one part, but arises from the
> whole human organism for movement. By suppressing
> such a movement, I do what I need to enable me to
> understand a definite thing expressed in words by
> another man. I understand what he says not by
> performing this movement, but by suppressing it, by only
> stimulating the organism for movement in me — as far as
> the finger tips, so to say — and then holding it back,
> stopping it. By suppressing the movement, I comprehend
> what is spoken.[25]

Here we are given a foundation for an understanding of the function of the word sense. We are shown that it is the movement that is not executed, the gesture that does not express itself, that conveys the understanding of the word addressed to us. The non-accomplished intention, which eliminates itself *in statu nascendi* and keeps still instead of moving, is the basis of our word sense.

This occurrence can be compared with resonance. When I sing a certain sequence of tones into the piano, they echo back softly. This does not happen when the strings are in vibration, but only when they are at rest. In the same way the spoken word resounds in me when I suppress the movement of its gesture instead of executing it. This happens only through that organ called the pyramidal system, that complex bundle of countless nerves that acts like a damper or mute. It does not execute the voluntary movement but holds it back, thus becoming the instrument in which the spoken word finds its echo or resonance. Understanding the word is the result.

Now we also see why the threshold of the small child's understanding of speech is higher than that of speaking. This was indicated when the development of speech was described. At the end of the first year the child has learned, with the help of the pyramidal system he has developed, to suppress certain gesture movements, and thus has advanced to the understanding of words. He still has not learned speech itself, however, because the understanding of words, the acquisition of the word sense, is a necessary prerequisite for the formation of the motor activity of speaking, that it, the speech movement itself. As long as the child babbles, he has not developed a word sense. The gradual transformation of babbling into speaking occurs only after this development. This must be clearly seen, otherwise, we cannot fully understand the growth of the child's mind. The sense of speech is born through the acquisition of the ability to walk upright, and only through the birth of the sense of speech can speaking unfold.

Rudolf Steiner has often indicated that speaking is formed from the entire voluntary motor activity. In his lecture from which we have been quoting, he describes it in the following way:

> On exploring the human being with the methods of spiritual science we find that the basis for understanding words is closely allied to the basis for speech ... Speech arises out of the soul life, is enkindled in the soul life through the will. Without our willing it, without the development of a will impulse, naturally no spoken word can arise. If one observes the human being with spiritual scientific means, one sees that when he speaks there

occurs in him a process similar to what occurs when he understands something spoken. But when the human being himself speaks, a much smaller portion of his organism, much less of his organism of movement or motor organism, is embraced. That means that the whole motor organism is concerned as sense of speech, as word sense. The whole motor organism is at the same time the sense of speech. A part of it comes into prominence and is set in motion by the soul when we speak. This part of the motor organism has its chief organ in the larynx, and speech is the stimulation of movements in the larynx through impulses of will. What happens in the larynx through one's own speech is that will impulses emerge from the soul and set in motion the organ of movement concentrated in the system of the larynx, whereas for the perception of words our entire motor organism is the sense organ.[26]

Steiner here points to the fact that the 'motor organism,' the resting part of which (the pyramidal system) we have recognized as the organ of the sense of speech, bears speech most intimately within it. The speech process, however, is concentrated in the speech organs, which arrange themselves around the larynx, and the muscles of tongue, cheeks, jaw and larynx are activated within the motor organism.

The physical organ of the sense of thought

Our considerations have reached the point at which we can say that in the course of the child's speech development, the thought sense unfolds. It happens during the second year and the relation of the formation of the thought sense to the acquisition of speech is similar to the relation of the formation of the word sense to the acquisition of the ability to walk upright. In our search for the organ of the thought sense can we conclude that the connection of this organ to the speech organs is similar to the intimate connection of the organ of the speech sense with motor ability? To arrive at an answer, we must examine the nerve supply of the larynx and its complicated muscular apparatus.

The muscles of the larynx present a kind of muscular system in miniature, and in their manifoldness and complexity of arrangement, they make possible all the finer movements necessary for the act of speaking. The muscles of the abdomen, chest, back and limbs are reduced in number and size in the larynx and they are also simplified and drawn together as if in a knot. Yet they render possible the endless variety of muscular combinations needed for the production of the singing and speaking voice in all its modulation. This motor system in miniature is supplied by two major nerve branches that come from above and below. They penetrate the larynx in pairs on both its right and left sides where they branch out to connect with the muscles and other tissues.

Physiologists have lost their sense of wonder for the fact that these two nerve branches are stems of the vagus nerve, which is one of the twelve cranial nerves. The vagus is special among the cranial nerves because it alone belongs to the autonomic nervous system. This is the plexus that is spread out over the body and regulates the large organs, the blood vessels and the circulation of fluids through the tissues. Its function mainly controls those processes occurring in the subconscious. The excretions of the large glands, the heartbeat, the muscular movements of stomach and intestines, the tension of blood vessels are all governed by the autonomic nervous system. What goes on in this dim realm is regulated by the vagus nerve and is brought to our waking consciousness only when conditions of illness become known through pain, discomfort and sensations like hunger and thirst. It is from this nerve, which belongs to the vegetative layers of our existence, that branches pass to the larynx and regulate speech, one of the highest of human achievements.

This most extraordinary phenomenon demands our full attention. Speaking is an entirely voluntary, motor act and yet, in contrast to all other voluntary movements, it is not bound to the nerves of the pyramidal system. On the contrary, important as it is to human existence, through its nerve supply it belongs to the dull vegetative strata. This can be explained by the fact that the larynx is not part of the muscular apparatus but belongs to the respiratory system. To say this, however, only bridges the abyss produced by the problems of this form complex. The abyss itself remains unexplored. Yet, an understanding of this strange phenomenon should be sought.

In a beautiful essay Rudolf Treichler has shown that the totality of the autonomic nervous system is intimately connected with the sense of life and that one is even justified in speaking of this nervous system as the organ of perception for the sense of life.[27] We can, therefore, ascribe to the totality of our manifestations and processes of life the realm of the vegetative or autonomic system, from which certain sensations, such as hunger and thirst, comfort and discomfort and other bodily sensations reach the threshold of consciousness.

In the lecture mentioned above in which Rudolf Steiner tries to describe the organs of the three highest senses, he also devotes a passage to the organ of the sense of thought:

> What is the organ of perception for the thoughts of another? Inasmuch as we are aware of life and animation within us, it is all that we are. If, then, you reflect that you have life throughout your whole organism and that this life is a unity, then the living animation of the entire organism, to the extent it expresses its life in the physical, is the organ for the thoughts that come to us from outside ... If we were not endowed with life, we could not perceive the thoughts of another. I am not here speaking of the sense of life. We are not concerned with the inner perception of our own life because this belongs to the sense of life. But insofar as we bear life within us, everything in us that is physical organism of that life forms the organ of perception for the thoughts directed toward us by another person.[28]

These indications of Rudolf Steiner clearly show that he saw the organ of the sense of thought in the region of 'activity' and 'life' in us, in those regions that belong to the autonomic nervous system. Can we imagine that this weaving of constructive and destructive life processes is itself the organ of the sense of thought? Steiner makes a definite reservation here when he says, and even repeats, that he mans life 'insofar as it expresses itself in the physical' or 'everything in us that is the physical organism of that life.' How should this be understood?

Thorough research has gradually led physiologists and neurologists to distinguish two different parts of the autonomic nervous system — a sympathetic and a parasympathetic region. Quite different functions, which are polar opposites, are attributed to them. The sympathetic system exerts a stimulating effect and the parasympathetic system a calming one. A host of theories and assumptions have been built upon these polar functions of the autonomic nervous system. Hess, who has spent his life with these questions, formulates it thus: 'The sympathetic system serves the unfolding of actual energy, the parasympathetic the restitution and preservation of potential productivity.'[29] Treichler characterizes this polarity in his essay in the following way: 'It should be mentioned that the parasympathetic system, which includes the vagus nerve, serves more the perception of form conditions, while the sympathetic system perceives and communicates the activities of the organs.'[30]

This is a formulation that shows the way to the solution of our problem. The formation of theories about the functions of the vegetative nervous system suffers today from a fatal error. Invariably, an active, motor effect is ascribed to these nerves and the fact that they are purely sensory, sensing organs is almost entirely overlooked. When Treichler assigns a sensitivity for the life activities of the organs to the sympathetic system, he may well have found the right interpretation of it. The sympathetic system is the organ of the sense of life. But what is meant by the 'perception of form conditions?'

Rudolf Steiner has shown that around the seventh year the child experiences a decisive metamorphosis of his life forces. Until then they have been devoted almost exclusively to plastically formative activity in the organism, when they were forming the structure and shape of the organs and tissues. But at the time of the second dentition a part of these formative forces is set free and transformed into those forces needed by our thinking for its activity. What Treichler calls 'perception of form conditions' and associates with the vagus nerve, belongs to those plastically formative life forces that are later active as thought forces.

Can we not dare, on the basis of everything we have presented thus far, to assign to the vagus nerve with all its many branches passing through the whole living organism, the role of the organ of the sense of thought? This nerve is indeed the 'physical' part, the part permanently retained in a material way, of all life processes performed in our organism. Just as the sympathetic part of the autonomic nervous system is the organ of the sense of life, so the parasympathetic part, which is connected with the brain via the vagus nerve, is the organ of the sense of thought.

Thus, light is thrown on the phenomenon that was the starting point of our deliberations. The muscles of the larynx, as voluntary organs, are supplied from two pairs of nerves branching off from the trunk of the vagus nerve. Now we come to understand why the sense of thought is formed along with the development of speech during the second year. After the child acquires the word sense, he becomes conscious of the surrounding sphere of language. Until then he perceived words and sentences merely as signs for sounds and noises, but now for the first time he begins to understand what is expressed in the spoken word. He also begins to imitate the words and sentences he perceives and to use his larynx for the activity of speaking. For it is not the nerve impulses that make use of the larynx as speech organ, but the soul itself preparing to speak. Thereby, the speech organ and its muscles, as well as the corresponding nerves, are permeated by the attempts at sound formation continually being made by the child. The muscles gradually come under the domination of the speaking soul and the word images stream through the corresponding nerves into the whole autonomic nervous system.* There they merge with the life activities of the

---

* The concept of the total autonomic nervous system as an anatomical physiological unity is today generally accepted. Stöhr, for example, writes: 'Results of anatomical investigations justify the assumption that the whole of the sympathetic system is a closed one, from which the outermost parts are sunk as independent little branches into the epithelial gland and muscle cells which they have to supply and form an inseparable physiological and anatomical unit or they complete their course as differently shaped sensitive terminals.'

whole organism and imprint it with the characteristics of his native language. Man is deeply influenced in all his life processes by the effects of the language in whose sphere he grows up and lives. This comes about along the path we have just described.

The word forms that are counted among the life processes flow in and stream along the path of the nerves. They also work through the vagus nerve with all its ramifications and in this way transform it into an organ that can act as the physical apparatus for the activity of the sense of thought.

The formative forces active in the life processes are identical with those that have built up all living forms in the world. They work in nature as well as in man, and thus are part of the eternal ideas that form all life and being. When they meet with the forms of words and sounds, the way leading through the gate of the word is opened to the ideas themselves.

We have called the pyramidal system a musical instrument with many thousands of strings that enable us to perceive speech, and we can call the vagus nerve as form the sum total of all that is active in us as life organism. This realm is the sphere of the creative ideas that hold sway in the living organism, form-creating and form-destroying. We can look upon this life sphere as a mighty brain, not fixed in shape, but being formed ever anew in the stream of life and deeds. The twigs and branches of the vagus nerve rise from it, combine with each other, and converge like the twigs and branches in the crown of a tree to form the trunk. But here the trunk rises from below upward and plunges its roots into the other brain that is enclosed as physical structure in the skull. The vagus nerve passes from the living interplay of the organs into the dead and rigidly formed brain. On this bridge between life and death the organ of the sense of thought is formed ever anew. The ideas and concepts brought to us through the words of other human beings meet in the vagus nerve the living formative forces that are active in the life organism of man. From this meeting arises the immediate cognition characteristic of all sense processes. It can enter the sphere of consciousness because the vagus nerve has such a close anatomical connection with the brain. Thus, the ideas contained in the word images can be recognized and experienced in our waking consciousness.

These phenomena now make possible a beginning for the understanding of the morphological manifestation that finds its expression in the nerve supply of the larynx. Here the parasympathetic nervous system, to the extent that the vagus nerve is involved in it, is revealed as the sense organ of the sense of thought.★

The Ego Sense

The knowledge gained in the last section of this chapter can be summarized as follows:

1. In the course of the first year the child acquires the sense of speech in connection with the ability to walk upright.
2. The development of the sense of speech begins in the second year and opens the sphere of the word to the child.
3. The sense of thought is developed in the course of learning to speak.

With the awakening of the sense of thought in the third year, the child opens himself to the thoughts communicated to him through the words of other people. As a climax of this development, we discovered that the child could call himself by the term, 'I.' He thereby crossed the threshold of the third year.

In a later presentation of his theory of the senses, Rudolf Steiner adds the ego sense to the senses of speech and of thought, and characterizes it in the following way: 'It is not a question here that one knows of one's own ego, but that one confronts another person whose ego becomes revealed. The ego sense perceives the ego of the other. That is the ego sense, not that one perceives one's own ego.'[31]

An especially detailed description of how the ego sense functions was given by Rudolf Steiner at the occasion of the founding of the Waldorf School. There he said:

★ In this Section I have refrained quite intentionally from discussing the exposition given by H.E. Lauer in the fifth chapter of his fundamental book on the *Twelve Senses of Man*. There an attempt is also made to describe the physical organs of the 'higher' senses. Such a discussion here would become needlessly long and would be of interest to only a limited number of the readers for whom this book is meant.

If you meet another person, the following occurs: For a
short period you perceive a person, and he or she makes
an impression upon you. That impression disturbs you
inwardly; you feel that the person, a being comparable to
yourself, makes an impression upon you like an attack.
The result is that you 'defend' yourself inwardly, you
resist this attack and become inwardly aggressive toward
the person. In this aggression you become crippled, and
the aggression ceases. Then the other person can again
make an impression upon you, and after you thus have
time to regain you aggressive strength, you carry out
another act of aggression. This is the relationship that
exists when one person meets another and perceives the
other I — that is devotion to the other — inner
resistance; sympathy–antipathy ...

However, there is still something else. As sympathy
develops, you go to sleep in the other person; as antipathy
develops, you wake up, and so forth. In the vibrations of
meeting another person, there is a rapid alternation
between waking and sleeping. We have to thank the organ
of the I-sense that this can occur. This organ of I-sensing
is so formed that it explores the I of another person, not
wakefully but in its sleeping will, and then quickly
delivers the results of this sleepy exploration to cognition,
that is, to the nervous system.[32]

Here we see clearly the two-phase character of ego perception,
which seems to function like a breathing process become
inward. With this two-phase nature the period in the child's
development can be indicated, at least in passing, during which
the child begins to unfold his ego sense. During the first two
years the child is primarily a being reacting 'sympathetically'
toward other people. Especially if he is not spoiled, the child is
full of confidence toward other people and seldom feels discomfort toward strangers. An infant may often be hesitant when
meeting others and may feel fear or anxiety toward strangers, but
once he has overcome his shyness, he will throw himself into the
other being, fully of sympathy. He 'sleeps' into the other one.

E. Köhler writes about her Annie at the age of two years and six months, 'Annie wants to be sociable. Children of different ages attract her attention. When she sees a child in the street, she stops, runs toward him, gives him her hand and wants to kiss him. Frightened mothers and nurse maids often pull their children away and look unkindly at Annie. She does not feel this mistrust.'[33] In the meeting with other egos this child is still entirely clothed in sympathy and does not confront them 'consciously,' which means that she has not yet developed the alternation between sympathy and antipathy in the realm of the ego sense.

For this age there hardly exists any difference between man, animal and object. All things in the surrounding world are equal in action as well as in suffering. Thus, Annie can say that her toy rabbit will watch her eating, while the next day it will be the orange that lies on the table that will watch her. Children, therefore, have pity for things as well as people, and a broken biscuit can bring them as easily to tears as a mother who must lie in bed with a headache. I remember a little three-year-old melancholic who, when we all sat at table, suddenly broke into bitter tears. He gradually let us know that it was the chair standing so lonely and unused against the wall that caused him such great misery.

Such behaviour is not connected with the fact that the infant treats all things anthropomorphically, as superficial psychology would have it. It is rather the other way around, and everything is felt uniformly without life and soul. It, therefore, can be pitied, feared, mothered and embraced with sympathy. W. Hansen quite rightly says:

> A separation between subject and object does not yet exist for the child in the sense that the subject has consciousness through the knowledge of the object from which he differs. From the fact that he applies names used for soul qualities such as thinking, being good, expecting, enjoying, etc., also to his animal, plant and material surroundings, we are justified in drawing only one conclusion: That the child does not yet separate these domains of the world from those of the ensouled human being, nor does he

draw a line between different realms of existence. He
thinks and reacts toward everything in the same way.[34]

This illustrates clearly that the ego sense has not yet developed
in the infant. Otherwise, he could immediately differentiate
between man and the other beings and things of his environment. The child embraces everything with a certain amount of
sympathy, which means he sleeps into things and beings without being able to meet them in the recoil of the awakening
antipathy. This process of waking up does not occur until about
the time of the first period of defiance. Between the third and
fourth years, the child begins to oppose the surrounding world
for the first time, and to put his own will antipathetically over
against his environment. Everything that until this point had
been easy and possible without fuss, now comes about under
difficulties and with arguments. The child wants to do everything himself — to dress and undress by himself, to decide independently how to play and often to do exactly the opposite of
what grown-ups would like him to do. During this time, his
first conflicts with his mother, brothers and sisters occur
because the child becomes aware of his own independent being
quite differently from before.

The significant meeting, about which we spoke in the third
chapter, has taken place. The eternal individuality of the child
was called the awakener of the sleeping thinking, and we said,
'At the moment when both behold each other and confront each
other eye to eye, the consciousness of one's own ego awakens
for the first time.' This process of becoming conscious is the
cause of the first period of defiance.

Remplein describes this stage concretely. He says,

Behind the child's outer rejection of the play community
stands an important development of the ego
consciousness ... The ego centre, which hitherto had only
registered all experiences without becoming conscious of
itself, now becomes the object of experience. At the same
time the symbiotic unity of child and world falls apart
and a first separation occurs between ego and non-ego.

> This transition happens without deliberation or self-reflection. In action and in meeting the world the child becomes conscious of himself.[35]

This process makes it possible for the 'sympathetic' attitude of the child to become ambivalent and for the child to bring distinctly antipathetic features into the fabric of his experiences. It is not fear, anxiety, shame or repulsion of anything alien that puts him into opposition to his environment. It is rather the awakening consciousness of his self that leads him into an attitude of defiance. It is a truly positive phase of development that starts here and it should be valued as such by parents and teachers. The child wakes up to the consciousness of his own self and does not want to lose this awakening again. Therefore, he becomes defiant.

Along with meeting the other person with sympathy, the attitude of defiance enables the child to acquire rejection also because only in the continuous alternation between these two phases of the soul can the ego sense develop. This development, however, does not seem to progress as quickly and as directly as that of the senses of speech and thought. The ego sense needs a long period of development for its complete unfolding.

In the third chapter we pointed out the 'radical difference' between walking and speaking on the one hand and thinking on the other. In a similar way there also exists a radical difference between the senses of speech and thought and the ego sense. Though the awakening thinking is a necessary presupposition for the gradual development of the ego sense, this highest sense does not unfold along with the development of thinking in the same way that the senses of speech and thought were formed during the acquisition of the ability to walk upright and of speech. The development of thinking may certainly produce the awakening of the ego consciousness, but this is not the ego sense. Only a being who has gained full consciousness of his own ego can as a consequence of this develop an ego sense.

The acquisition of thought may well become the mirror of the ego in which the latter then begins to experience itself. This self-experience makes possible the antipathetic attitude essential for the forming of the ego sense. The meeting of two ego conscious beings results in those two phases, the sympathetic as well as the antipathetic impulses, which lead to an immediate experience of the other ego. Up to now, detailed observations in this field of child development hardly exist. One can, however, assume that in shape and appearance, the father is the most important stimulator for the development of the ego sense. He becomes a symbol of the surrounding world that confronts the child, not protecting like the mother, but demanding.

The formation of the ego sense is not completed until the ninth year. It is consolidated at this threshold of the child's development and Rudolf Steiner has called particular attention to it. He describes this time of transformation in the following way:

> In the ninth year the child experiences what is really a complete transformation in his soul, indicating a significant change in his bodily-physical experience. From then on, the child begins to experience himself as separate from his surroundings. He learns to distinguish between world and self. When we are able to observe rightly, we must say that before this revolution in human consciousness, world and self flow more or less together. From the ninth year (this is of course meant approximately) man distinguishes between himself and the world. This must be thoroughly taken into account in the teaching material and educational life that we bring to the child from the ninth year on. It will be well, up to this time, not to confuse the child with a description or characterization of things that are separated from man or can be regarded separately from man. You see, if we tell the child fables or fairy tales, we speak about animals or perhaps plants in the same way as we speak of people. Animals and plants are personified, and quite rightly, because the child does not yet distinguish between self and world, because

everywhere in the world the child sees something that
he experiences in himself.[36]

With the ninth year this experience changes radically. The formation of the ego sense is completed and the child learns
through the experience of this sense to differentiate between
man and the other beings of nature. The age of fairy tales and
legends comes to an end. Parents and teachers are observed
critically and the ego begins to measure itself against other
egos. The awakening into the sphere of personality has set in.
What began with the first age of defiance has now reached its
conclusion.

On two occasions Rudolf Steiner spoke about the sense
organ underlying the ego sense. One passage reads as follows:
'The organ for perceiving the I spreads over the entire human
being and consists of a very subtle substance. For that reason,
people do not speak of an organ for perceiving another's I.'[37]

In the second passage he speaks much more extensively
about this sense organ.

> Ego perception has its own organ, just like the perception
> of sight or sound. Only, while this organ has its starting
> point in the head, it is formed by all the rest of the body
> as well insofar as that body depends on the head. The
> whole man, understood as organ of perception, and as he
> is sensibly-physically constructed, is really an organ of
> perception for the ego of another. One might also say
> that, insofar as it has the whole man dependent on it and
> rays its faculty of ego perception throughout the entire
> man, the organ of perception for the ego of another is the
> head. Man at rest, man as a stationary human form with
> the head as its centre, is the perceptive organ for the ego
> of another man. Thus the organ of perception for the ego
> is the largest perceptive organ we have, and we ourselves
> as physical man are this organ.[38]

Little can be added to such a description because it is manifest
that the entire human body, 'insofar as that body depends on the

head,' is the organ of perception for the ego sense. Until about the ninth year, however, the child grows directly through the forces of the head. During infancy the head is still overly large in comparison with the rest of the body and this disproportion is harmonized only gradually, especially between the third and ninth years. The limbs stretch, the trunk of the body grows larger and the head lags behind in growth. As a result, the particularly well-formed body structure arises that children have around the ninth year. From infant form through the first 'change of form' occurring between the seventh and eighth years, that 'shape before puberty,' which in its architecture shows such perfect harmony, has come about.

The attainment of this shape of the body really depends on the head, whose growth stands in closest connection with the function of two inner secretory glands of the brain, the pineal gland or epiphysis, and the pituitary gland or hypophysis. The working together of these two glands regulates the forces of growth and form in such a way that they lead to a harmonious or disharmonious development of the body. The equilibrium between epiphysis and hypophysis results in the harmonious shape of the nine-year-old child. Before this time the activity of the epiphysis predominates, later that of the hypophysis. The development of this perfect bodily form, which is corrupted only later in puberty, coincides with the attainment of the ego sense. During this stage man has reached the highest level of his physical development. He has become the true image of man who has also unfolded the highest sense, the ego sense. In a certain sense, this is also the beginning of a descent because, during pre-puberty and maturity, the body and limbs become earthbound and lose that touch for the other world that they still retained until about the ninth year. The growing human being falls prey to the earth, becomes heavy, burdened and worried about his path of destiny.

He has, however, gained the ego sense, and this he is allowed to keep and carry with him as a lifelong gift from this time onward. The senses of speech and thought likewise remain with him as gifts through which he can approach the spirit of all existence. Through the sense of speech all treasures of the word are opened. Through the sense of thought the wisdom of all past and present creation is unveiled. Through the sense of ego he can recognize the other man as his brother. Thus, childhood has endowed him with a possession never to be lost.

Walking, speaking and thinking have made him a man. They have raised him from a creature to a being who can recognize himself. The senses of speech, thought and ego on the other hand help him to approach the spirit depths of all existence. They open paths into higher worlds that lie beyond the world of the senses. In those three highest senses the sphere of the senses begins to abolish itself and points the way to its own overcoming. This is a sacrifice because it leads to annihilation. Further on, a resurrection is waiting. The sense world will break asunder and a spirit world will open up beyond.

Getrost, das Leben schreitet
Zum ew'gen Leben hin;
Von inn'rer Glut geweitet
Verklärt sich unser Sinn.

Our life with courage ending
Eternal life draws near,
With inner glow expanding
Transfigured sense grows clear.

Die Sternwelt wird zerfliessen
Zum goldnen Lebenswein,
Wir werden sie geniessen
Und lichte Sterne sein.[39]

The star world now is flowing
As living golden wine,
Its joys on us bestowing,
Ourseves as stars shall shine

(Novalis)

Notes

Chapter 1.
1. Stern, *Psychology of Early Childhood*, p. 69.
2. Magnus & de Kleijn, 'Körperstellung, Gleichgewicht und Bewegung.'
3. Stifter, *Betrachtungen und Bilder.*
4. Stern, *Psychology of Early Childhood*, p. 124.
5. Portmann, *Biologische Fragmente.*
6. Storch, *Die Sonderstellung des Menschen.*
7. Portmann, *Biologische Fragmente*, p. 72.
8. Steiner, *Spiritual Guidance.*
9. Steiner, *Karma of Untruthfulness*, lecture of Dec. 21, 1916.

Chapter 2.
1. Portmann, *Biologische Fragmente*, p. 74.
2. Steiner, *Metamorphoses of the Soul*, lecture of Jan. 20, 1910.
3. Gehlen, *Der Mensch*, p. 208.
4. See also below, Chapter 3, Section 3, for the quotation of Rudolf Steiner.
5. Bühler, *The Mental Development of the Child.*
6. Kainz, *Psychologie der Sprache*, Vol. 2, p. 3.
7. Porzig, *Das Wunder der Sprache*, p. 54.
8. Kainz, *Psychologie der Sprache*, Vol. 2, p. 4.
9. Stern, *Psychology of Early Childhood.*
10. Stern, *Psychology of Early Childhood*, p. 141.

11. Kainz, *Psychologie der Sprache.* Vol. 2, p. 35.
12. Steiner, *Metamorphoses of the Soul*, lecture of Jan. 20, 1910.
13. Hamann, *Des Ritters von Rosencreuz letzte Willensmeinung.*

Chapter 3.
1. W. Köhler, *The Mentality of Apes.*
2. Bühler, *The Mental Development of the Child.*
3. Remplein, *Die seelische Entwicklung in der Kindheit und Reifezeit.*
4. As quoted by Remplein, *Die seelische Entwicklung in der Kindheit und Reifezeit.*
5. I have based my descriptions on the account in Homeyer, *Von der Sprache zu den Sprachen.*
6. E. Köhler, *Die Persönlichkeit des dreijährigen Kindes.*
7. Steiner, *The Realm of Language*, lecture of July 17, 1915.
8. E. Köhler, *Die Persönlichkeit des dreijährigen Kindes.*
9. Steiner, *Building Stones*, lecture of April 12, 1917.
10. Steiner, *Die Wissenschaft vom Werden des Menschen*, lecture of Sep. 2, 1918.
11. Steiner, *World History in the Light of Anthroposophy*, lecture of Dec. 24, 1923.
12. Steiner, *World History in the Light of Anthroposophy*, lecture of Dec. 24, 1923.
13. Stern in his *Psychology of Early Childhood* gives an explanation of

marking and be-thinking different from the above. It would lead us too far afield if we went into details here.

14. Bühler, *The Mental Development of the Child*, p. 314.

15. Stern, *Psychology of Early Childhood*, p. 207.

16. Stern, *Psychology of Early Childhood*, p. 240.

17. Steiner, *Foundations of Human Experience*, lecture of Aug. 22, 1919, p. 55.

18. Stern, *Psychology of Early Childhood*, p. 276.

19. Stern, *Psychology of Early Childhood*.

20. E. Köhler, *Die Persönlichkeit des dreijährigen Kindes*, p. 67.

21. Stern, *Psychology of Early Childhood*, p. 170.

22. E. Köhler, *Die Persönlichkeit des dreijährigen Kindes*, p. 67.

23. Rauch, *Der Schatten des Vaters*.

24. Reichard, *Die Früherinnerung*.

25. Reichard, *Die Früherinnerung*.

26. Busemann, 'Erregungsphasen der Jugend.'

27. E. Köhler, *Die Persönlichkeit des dreijährigen Kindes*, p. 232.

28. Steiner, *Spiritual Guidance*, p. 8.

29. Remplein, *Die seelische Entwicklung in der Kindheit und Reifezeit*, p. 143.

30. Steiner, *The Spiritual Guidance of Mankind*, p. 9.

31. Steiner, *The Spiritual Guidance of Mankind*, p. 18f.

Chapter 4.

1. W. Stern, *Psychology of Early Childhood*, p. 147.

2. Scheler, *Abhandlungen und Aufsätze*, Vol. 1, p. 329ff.

3. Binswanger, *Ausgewählte Vorträge und Aufsätze*, Vol. 2. p. 308.

4. Steiner, *The Wisdom of Man,* lecture of October 23, 1909.

5. Steiner, *Von Seelenrätseln.*

6. Valentine, *The Psychology of Early Childhood*, p. 393.

7. Valentine, *The Psychology of Early Childhood*, p. 399.

8. Preyer, *Die Seele des Kindes*, p. 306.

9. Stern, *Psychology of Early Childhood*, p. 146.

10. Preyer, *Die Seele des Kindes*, p. 308.

11. Steiner, *Anthroposophie, Ein Fragment*, p. 93.

12. Valentine, *The Psychology of Early Childhood*, p. 414.

13. Steiner, *Anthroposophie, Ein Fragment*, p. 94.

14. Stern, *Psychology of Early Childhood*, p. 165.

15. Steiner, *Anthroposophie, Ein Fragment*, p. 94.

16. Valentine, *The Psychology of Early Childhood*, p. 420.

17. Quoted from Kainz, *Psychologie der Sprache*, Vol. 2, p. 52.

18. Quoted from Schmitt, 'Helen Keller und die Sprache.'

19. See also K. König, 'Die Geistgestalt Helen Kellers.'

20. Steiner, *Von Seelenrätseln*, p. 225.

21 .See also the detailed expositions by the author, 'Der Motorische Nerv wird entthront.' and 'Die Nerventätigkeit.'

22. Steiner, *Die geistigen Hintergründe*, lecture of Sep. 2, 1916.

23. Steiner, *Die geistigen Hintergründe*, lecture of Sep. 2, 1916.

24. Conrad, 'New Problems of Aphasia.'

25. Steiner, *Die geistigen Hintergründe*, lecture of Sep. 2, 1916.

26. Steiner, *Die geistigen Hintergründe*, lecture of Sep. 2, 1916.

27. Treichler, 'Von der Welt des Lebenssinnes.'

28. Steiner, *Die geistigen Hintergründe,* lecture of Sep. 2, 1916.
29. Quoted from Kroetz, 'Allgemeine Physiologie der autonomen nervösen Correlationen.'
30. Treichler, 'Von der Welt des Lebenssinnes.'
31. Steiner, *Weltwesen und Ichheit,* June 20, 1916.
32. Steiner, *Foundations of Human Experience,* lecture of Aug. 29, 1919, p. 140.
33 E. Köhler, *Die Persönlichkeit des dreijährigen Kindes,* p. 110.
34. Hansen, *Die Entwicklung des kindlichen Weltbildes,* p. 211.
35. Remplein, *Die seelische Entwicklung in der Kindheit und Reifezeit,* p. 145.
36. Steiner, *The Renewal of Education,* lecture of April 3, 1920.
37. Steiner, *Foundations of Human Experience,* lecture of Aug. 29, 1919, p. 139.
38. Steiner, *Die geistigen Hintergründe,* lecture of Sep. 2, 1916.
39. Novalis, *Hymns to the Night.*

Bibliography

Binswanger, L. *Ausgewählte Vorträge und Aufsätze,* Vol. 2. Bern 1955.

Brock, J. *Biologische Daten für den Kinderarzt,* Vol. 2, Berlin 1934.

Bühler, K. *The Mental Development of the Child.* London 1930.

Busemann, A. 'Erregungsphasen der Jugend,' *Zeitschrift für Kinderforschung,* No. 33. 1927.

Conrad, K. 'New Problems of Aphasia,' *Brain,* Vol. 77, 1954.

Gehlen, A. *Der Mensch. Seine Natur und seine Stellung in der Welt,* Bonn 1950.

Hamann, *Des Ritters von Rosencreuz letzte Willensmeinung.*

Hansen, W. *Die Entwicklung des kindlichen Weltbildes,* Munich 1949.

Homeyer, H. *Von der Sprache zu den Sprachen,* Olten 1947.

Kainz, F. *Psychologie der Sprache.* Vol. 2. Stuttgart 1943.

Köhler, E. *Die Persönlichkeit des dreijährigen Kindes,* Leipzig 1936.

Köhler, W. *The Mentality of Apes,* London/New York 1927.

König, K. 'Die Geistgestalt Helen Kellers,' Das seelenpflege-bedürftige Kind, Vol. 3, No. 1, 1956.

—, 'Der Motorische Nerv wird entthront.' *Die Drei,* No. 1, 1955.

—, 'Die Nerventätigkeit kann nur durch eine Methode der Ausschliessung erfasst werden,' *Beiträge zu einer Erweiterung der Heilkunst,* No. 3/4, 1955.

Kroetz, C. 'Allgemeine Physiologie der autonomen nervösen Correlationen,' *Handbuch der normalen und pathologischen Physiologie,* Vol. 16, No. 2, Berlin 1931.

Magnus, A. & de Kleijn, A. Körperstellung, Gleichgewicht und Bewegung. *Handbuch der normalen und pathologischen Psychologie,* Vol. 15.1, Berlin 1930.

Novalis, *Hymns to the Night,* Translated by Mabel Cotterell.

Portmann, A. *Biologische Fragmente zu einer Lehre vom Menschen,* Basel 1944.

Porzig, W. *Das Wunder der Sprache,* Bern 1950.

Preyer, W. *Die Seele des Kindes,* Leipzig 1900.

Rauch, K. *Der Schatten des Vaters,* Esslingen 1954.

Reichard, H. *Die Früherinnerung,* Halle 1926.

Remplein, H. *Die seelische Entwicklung in der Kindheit und Reifezeit,* Munich 1950.

Scheler, M. *Abhandlungen und Aufsätze,* Vol. 1. Leipzig 1915.

Schmitt, A. 'Helen Keller und die Sprache,' *Münstersche Forschungen,* No.8, Münster 1954.

Sigismund, R. *Kind und Welt,* Braunschweig 1897.

Steiner, Rudolf, *Anthroposophy (A Fragment),* (Translated from German Complete Works (GA) No. 45), Anthroposophic Press, New York 1996.

—, *Building Stones for an Understanding of the Mystery of Golgotha,* (GA 175), Steiner Press, London 1972.

—, *The Foundations of Human Experience,* (formerly *Study of Man),* (GA 293), Anthroposophic Press, New York 1996.

—, *Die geistigen Hintergründe der menschlichen Geschichte,* (GA 170), Steiner Verlag, Dornach 1978.

—, *The Karma of Untruthfulness,* (GA 173), Vol. 1, Steiner Press, London 1988.

—, *Metamorphoses of the Soul,* (GA 59), Steiner Press, London 1983.

—, *The Realm of Language,* (from GA 162), Mercury Press, New York 1984.

—, *The Renewal of Education,* (GA 301), Steiner Schools Fellowship, Forest Row 1981.

—, *Spiritual Guidance of the Individual and Humanity,* (GA 15), Anthroposophic Press, New York 1992.

—, *Von Seelenrätseln,* (GA 21), Steiner Verlag, Dornach 1983.

—, *Weltwesen und Ichheit,* (GA 169), Steiner Verlag, Dornach 1963.

—, *The Wisdom of Man, of the Soul and of the Spirit,* (GA 115), Anthroposophic Press, New York 1971.

—, *Die Wissenschaft vom Werden des Menschen,* (GA 183), Dornach, 1967.

—, *World History in the Light of Anthroposophy,* (GA 233), Steiner Press, London 1977.

Stern, W. *Psychology of Early Childhood,* 2 ed., London 1930.

Stifter, Adalbert, *Betrachtungen und Bilder,* Vienna 1923.

Stöhr, *Mikroskopische Anatomie des vegetativen Nervensystems,* Berlin 1928.

Storch, O. *Die Sonderstellung des Menschen im Lebensabspiel und Vererbung,* Vienna 1948.

Treichler, R. 'Von der Welt des Lebenssinnes,' *Beiträge zur Erweiterung der Heilkunst,* No. 7/8, 1952.

Valentine, C.W. *The Psychology of Early Childhood,* London 1947.

Index

Brothers and Sisters

Karl König

'There can be no doubt that special traits of character and mental make-up are found in children and adults who belong to the different ranks in the order of birth.'

In this classic work from 1963, Karl König attempts to explain the various characteristics of first, second and third born people, without losing sight of the tremendous individuality of the human being. Just as our environment shapes our language, social behaviour and mannerisms, so our place in the family also determines how we encounter life.

This book is an invaluable handbook for parents, teachers and carers. Over the years it has become a definitive reference on the subject of child development.

Floris Books